Foreign Language Learning

A Linguistic Introduction

ROBERT L. POLITZER
Stanford University

Prentice-Hall, Inc.
Englewood Cliffs, New Jersey

Preface

This is a book about language and language learning. It discusses and tries to provide answers to three questions: (1) What is language? (2) What are the problems involved in foreign language learning? (3) What are the ways of dealing with these problems?

I hope that this book will be of interest to language teachers, educators, and parents of language students, but I want to emphasize that this is *not* primarily a book on how to *teach* foreign languages, but rather a discussion of how to *learn* them. The book is thus addressed primarily to *students* of foreign languages.

Each section of the book is followed by a series of "Learning Exercises," and some also include "Questions." The exercises give the reader the opportunity to check his comprehension of the material that has been presented, and the questions are used not only for the purpose of review but also to present some new material in question-and-answer form. Somewhat in the nature of programmed learning materials, the exercises and questions are immediately followed by the correct answers. We suggest that the reader try to do each exercise before looking at the answer, perhaps by covering the answer in the initial attempt.

The first three parts of the book attempt to create an understanding of language from the point of view of the learner of a
foreign language, but they are based entirely on English. In Part
IV, however, some of the material presented in question-and-answer
form provides applications of language learning problems to French,
Spanish, and German. Since the vast majority of modern foreign
language learners in this country are either studying or have at one
time studied one of these three languages, I hope that the sample
answers provided to the questions in Part IV will point the way
to a transfer of language learning skills acquired by the student to
his specific language learning situation. If this book is used in
conjunction with an elementary course in French, Spanish, or
German, the question-and-answer material of Part IV must of
course be introduced into the course at the discretion of the teacher.

The assumptions—some to be substantiated by specific research
—and the convictions on which this book is based are, in brief,
the following:

1. The language-learning ability of the mature language learner
   (high school age or older) can be increased by an understanding of the process of foreign language learning and by the
   creation of specific skills (understanding of patterning, sound-
   symbol relationship, etc.) which seem to underlie the ability
   to learn a foreign language.
2. There is a definite connection between the understanding of
   grammar as developed in the native language and the understanding of a foreign language. Until the advent of the new
   methods and curricula in foreign languages, it was generally
   felt that the grammatical categories of English were directly
   applicable to foreign languages. Linguists and many language
   teachers no longer hold this view. Nevertheless, the processes
   of linguistic analysis, the nature of sound-symbol relationship,
   the very nature of language itself, are the same for the native
   and for the foreign language. This book is thus based on the
   belief that there is a connection between English and any
   other language. It is, as a matter of fact, an attempt to establish—or re-establish—the connection between English and
   foreign language learning, which has often been lost sight of
   in the development of recent foreign language courses and
   curricula.

3. The important role assigned to foreign language learning in the high school and college curricula is not and should not be based solely on the acquisition of a skill. Of course the skill in itself is useful and opens up access to a foreign literature and culture, but at the same time the very process of acquiring the skill can be combined with creating a deeper understanding of the nature of language. Elementary language instruction and learning can have a subject matter content that goes beyond the acquisition of a skill alone.

4. Most high school and college students study a specific language without having any assurance that they are studying the language that they will ultimately need in their careers. It is thus of the utmost importance that language learning and teaching create an understanding of concepts that will be useful in the acquisition of other foreign languages.

In the new curriculum development that has taken place during recent years, the general emphasis—especially in mathematics and science on the high school level—has been on the creation of concepts and understanding of the subject matter rather than on the development of skills alone. Part of the reason for this stress on concepts has been the recognition of the simple fact that in a fast-moving world it seems more important to teach concepts that will facilitate the learning of whatever skills may be needed than to emphasize the creation of skills without accompanying understanding of concepts. One of the purposes of this book may thus be defined as an attempt to bring the initial stages of the foreign language learning experience in line with developments that have already taken place in other areas of the school curriculum.

One last word of warning and explanation: this book is thought to provide an experience that prepares or goes hand in hand with the experience of actually learning a foreign language. If it is used as a class text, much of the material in the book can and should be used as supplementary homework, especially in the initial stages of the course, in which often the present emphasis on audio-lingual training may make other types of homework difficult or problematical. The book would not and could not fulfill its purpose if it were treated by itself and for itself, dissociated from any past, present, or future foreign language learning experience. Learning *about* foreign language learning cannot take the place of foreign language learning itself, any more than the understanding of scientific or mathematical concepts can replace a knowledge of scientific and mathematical facts. Or to give an analogy from a less intellectual, but nonetheless important subject: just as the driver-training course and the few hours of behind-the-wheel experience that make up the driver training offered in most of our high schools will by themselves not produce a safe and experienced driver, so this book's theoretical discussion and few applications to French, Spanish, or German will not necessarily produce a successful and expert student of language. A good, safe driver is created by many hours of experience and practice. The knowledge of the foreign language is created in exactly the same way. But the driver-training course can—as experience has shown—contribute significantly to making the hours of practice more profitable. It can assure that practice will produce the right kind of experience. In a similar way, the material presented in this book will never change the fact that a foreign language can be acquired only through hours of training and practice; but I hope that our discussion of language and language learning methodology will help to make these hours of practice hours of the *right kind of practice*, and that it will enrich the foreign language learning experience by making it more interesting and profitable.

The present edition follows in all essential aspects the preliminary edition first published in 1964. The author wishes to express his gratitude for the many suggestions and comments which he received from numerous colleagues. Many of those suggestions have been incorporated into the present edition. It was not possible to take advantage of those suggestions which implied a fairly radical change of the original plan of this work, e.g., programming the entire text, adding extensive material concerning conflict of cultural patterns, and presenting the book in separate versions for students of French, German and Spanish. While in the opinion of the author all of these suggestions have great merit, carrying them out would imply profound changes in the concept of this work. These suggestions may very well form the basis for possible future publications distinct and separate from the present volume.

R.L.P.

Contents

Foreign

Language

Learning

I

Language
and
Language Learning

1

A General View

of Language

Languages are made up of organized sounds. The raw material of all languages are the sounds that the human voice is capable of producing. The infant—during the period that precedes his learning of the native language—produces most of these sounds, or is at least capable of producing them accidentally. But once the native language is learned, once the babbling of the infant has become speech, only the sounds of the native language are produced naturally and easily. From all the possible sounds the human voice can produce, each language makes a very limited selection. To the native speaker of the language these are the sounds that are natural and easy; to the foreigner they may be strange, complicated, difficult.

We may think of the thirty to sixty sound units (the number varies from language to language) that a language has chosen as the smallest units, or building stones, on which the language depends. All the other units of language—words, sentences, paragraphs, poems, speeches—are ultimately made up of different combinations and recombinations of these sound units. The principle according to which these sound units function is basically extremely simple: they function because they are different from each other, and because those who speak the language can perceive the difference. Thus you can hear that *pit* and *bit* are two different words because you can hear the difference between the sounds represented by the letters *p* and *b*—and you know that *bit* and *bid* are different because you can hear the difference between the sounds represented by the letters *t* and *d*. The fact that you can hear these differences and that /t/ and /d/ or /p/ and /b/ can make the distinction between different words proves that /p/, /b/, /t/, /d/ are sound units. (The technical name for those sound units is *phoneme*, and linguists use oblique lines / / whenever they refer to the phonemes of a language.)

If English is your native language, the fact that /t/, /d/, /p/, /b/ are sound units of English will not surprise you. In your native language, you have been conditioned to produce the sound units correctly and to hear the differences between them. As a matter of fact, your entire ability to understand spoken English depends ultimately on the fact that you can hear those differences in sound that are utilized according to the system of the English language. Other differences you learn to overlook. For instance, some of your friends or members of your family may pronounce /p/ or /b/ slightly differently from you or from each other, but you will recognize those differences as individual peculiarities, or most likely you will not pay any attention whatsoever. Or to give you a more precise example: watch carefully the way you pronounce the /p/ of *pin* and then notice the /p/ of *spin*. Actually there is a difference between the two /p/ sounds. The one of *pin* is pronounced with a very slight puff of air (technical name: *aspiration*) after it; the one of *spin* does not have that puff of air. The /p/ without the puff of air is normally produced only after /s/ in words like *spin*, *spot*, *spy*, etc. To you, as a native speaker of English, the /p/ of *pin* and that of *spin* will probably sound alike because the difference between the aspirated /p/ (let's write it p^h) and the nonaspirated one is *not* a significant (so-called *phonemic*) difference of English. Both /p/ sounds are simply variants (technical name: *allophones*) of the same sound unit (*phoneme*). The one without the puff of air occurs only after the *s*. Yet there are many languages in the world in which the /p/ of *pin* (the aspirate p^h) and that of *spin* (the unaspirate one: p) might be distinct sound units. In such languages, a word like *pita* may be opposed to a different word like *p^{h}ita*. And for speakers of such a language, the difference between /p/ (as in *spin*) and

/pʰ/ (as in *pin*) will be as obvious as the differences between /p/, /b/, /t/, /d/, etc. are to native speakers of English.

In addition to sound units like /p/, /t/, /b/, /d/, etc., there are also other sound features that belong to the inventory of basic sound units of any language. These are the sound features that make up the intonation, pitch, stresses, "sentence melodies," that are so characteristic of individual languages. Thus if you say the English word *pérmit* (stress on the first syllable), you have said a noun; but if you shift the stress to the second syllable, *permít*, you say a verb. This in itself proves how the stress can be significant (*phonemic*) in English. Or you might say *Charles is speaking English* in a matter-of-fact sort of way; but if Charles was a Frenchman and you didn't know that he spoke English, the statement *Charles is speaking English!* might become an exclamation. The whole intonation pattern of the sentence, the different pitches of your voice, might change to express your astonishment and surprise. Thus the pitch levels of your voice, the different ways in which they are arranged, are also significant (*phonemic*) features of English. Again, the very same features, like stress or pitch, may not be utilized or may be utilized very differently in different languages. Thus there are many languages (Chinese is one of them) in which pitch—or rather differences in pitch—finds the same kind of use that the differences between /p/, /b/, /t/, /d/, etc., find in English. In such languages (technically called *tone languages*) **ma** pronounced on a deep pitch may be a different word from *ma* on a medium or high pitch. (In Chinese, **ma** has four distinctly different meanings— *mother*, *horse*, *flax*, *curse*—depending on which of four tones it is pronounced with.) For speakers of those languages, these pitch (*tone*) differences will be obvious and easily recognizable, while the foreigner may not perceive them at all, or merely hear them as a funny kind of sing-song pattern superimposed upon the language.

The basic sound units of language are combined into larger units. The layman usually thinks of these larger units as words. Actually, they may be words, but more often than not they are smaller units that in turn make up words. Let us look at two sentences: *John thinks that this is impossible* and *Robert knows that this is incomprehensible.* Now let us ask: Which are the *smallest meaningful reusable* units of speech of which these sentences are made up? Some of these units are indeed words: *that, this, is, John;* but *Robert*—unlike *John*—can be subdivided further: the second syllable—*bert*—occurs with similar meaning (namely "ending of a masculine first name") in *Herbert*, *Albert*, and a few other names. *Thinks* and *knows* are composed of *think* and *know* plus the final *-s* which occurs in both of them and conveys in English the meaning of "third person singular present." *Incomprehensible* is divisible into several meaningful units: the first syllable *in-* carries the meaning of "negation." It is obviously a variant of the *im-* that starts the word *impossible*. The fact that *impossible* has *im-* while *incomprehensible* has *in-* is due to the simple fact that *im-* rather than *in-* is used before a /p/ or /b/. The *com-* of *comprehensible* reoccurs in words like *compound, compute, combine*, with the rather vague but still recognizable meaning of "together." In the word *comprehend* it can be replaced by units like *ap-, re-*, etc. (*apprehend, reprehend*). The unit *prehens* does not seem capable of further subdivision. It is reused in words like *apprehensive* and *comprehensive*. The ending of the word, finally, is obviously a unit that can be detached and used in many other adjectives, such as *legible, defensible, incorrigible*, etc.

The units of speech that we have been isolating are technically known as *morphemes*. They may be defined as the smallest building stones of language that have some sort of recognizable meaning or function. Some of these are words. Some are merely one sound (as the *-s* ending of *thinks, believes*, etc.). Some are syllable length. Some are polysyllabic. Thus the name of the state *Connecticut* (four syllables) is just one morpheme. It is impossible to take the name *Connecticut* and divide it up into any units that are reused or reusable in any way with the same meaning they have when they make up the name of the state.

For the professional linguist it is actually a lot easier to define the smallest building stones of meaning (the *morpheme*) than it is to define words. To say that the words are the units which are found in the dictionary, or those units that in writing are separated by spaces, does not give us a scientific definition that tells us very much about how these units function in speech. However, we can leave the problem of defining words to the linguist, and simply operate with the concept as it is understood traditionally. Words for us then are the units of meaning, made up minimally of one morpheme, which according to the feeling of native speakers are the units into which sentences and phrases are divisible. Unlike phonemes, which by themselves are meaningless, morphemes and words have meaning. Basically they have the power to convey meaning simply by virtue of being different from other sound symbols that convey different meanings. Typically at least, there is no necessary or intrinsic connection between the sounds of a morpheme or a word and the meaning that it conveys. In other words, we call a cow a *cow* because this is the word (or sequence of sounds) chosen by English for that particular animal. The connection between the symbol and the meaning for which it stands is purely conventional and arbitrary. Exceptions to this arbitrariness are few: thus if you call a dog a *bow-wow*, you might say that the name is *not* arbitrary—the sounds are an imitation of the dog's bark. Or—on a much higher level—if a poet chooses certain words containing certain sounds or uses certain rhymes because the sounds and rhythms are directly expressive of a certain mood, we can say that the symbols he uses are not arbitrary but directly motivated by the meaning that he wants to express. But by and large the principle of arbitrariness is basic and fundamental for all language. Certain sounds or sequences of sounds express certain ideas, because that is the way it has been decided on in a particular language. The question *why?* can usually be answered only in historical terms: in other words, we call a cow a *cow* because the Anglo-Saxons called it a *cu*, and so on.

We can thus compare language to some sort of construction set in which the smallest units, the phonemes, are combined into somewhat larger building stones that represent the morphemes, some of which can be combined and recombined to make still larger units (words). In discussing the next levels of language—namely the phrases and sentences that can be made up from the words—we can continue the analogy of the set of building stones. But we must think of phrases and sentences, not as larger building stones, but rather as constructions that can be built from words according to definite construction patterns or blueprints. The sentence *The father sees the child* thus follows a "pattern" of English. As a native speaker of English you know instinctively—even without grammatical instruction— that the sentence *The boy knows the answer* follows the same pattern. What do the two sentences have in common that enables us to say this? If we compare the sentences, we see that the elements in common are *The _____ _____-s the _____*. The blank spaces can be filled by other words: *The child finds the book; The teacher understands the* *problem*, etc. Even if we fill the blanks with nonsense syllables: *The mumak fabs the beema*, *The stoonce koobs the tibu*, etc., the nonsense sentences still convey the meaning that something or somebody is doing something to something or somebody else. Thus the pattern of the sentence is really the meaning conveyed by the grammatical relationships expressed in the sentence. In the sample sentence chosen, this grammatical meaning was expressed by the word *the*, by the sequence of the words employed, and by the ending (morpheme) -*s*. If we had replaced *the* by a nonsense word, left out the -*s*, our nonsense sentences would have ceased to communicate any meaning whatsoever: *Dla moomak fab gou beema* means nothing. It no longer conveys any recognizable grammatical relationship. Thus—at least so far as English is concerned—the pattern is expressed by precisely those elements which cannot be replaced by nonsense syllables without total loss of any sort of recognizable meaning. Those elements are *word order*, *grammatical endings*, and words of the type of *the*, *a*, *some*, etc., which express grammatical relationship and identify the word category of the following elements—the so-called *function* words.

Not all languages express grammatical patterns the same way. Word order and function words that are supremely important in English are, for instance, ordinarily not utilized at all in a language like Latin, at least not for the purpose of expressing grammatical relationships. *The father sees the child* is expressed by using the words **pater** (*father*), **puer** (*child, boy*), **videre** (*see*): **Puerum pater videt, Pater videt puerum,** etc., all mean the same thing. The permutation of the words changes the emphasis from **puerum** to **pater,** but not the basic meaning, which is expressed by the endings alone. If we want to say *The child sees the father*, we have to change the endings: **Puer patrem videt, Patrem videt puer,** etc.

2

The Problem

of Interference

Learning a language means learning a system or a code of the type that we have just discussed. Even in your native language you have not learned by memory all of the sentences that you ought to say or that you are ever going to say. What you have learned is a system and how to use it. Even in your native language it is of course possible to make mistakes and to misapply the system. A young child who says "I gived him the book" is not using the form *gived* because he has learned it from anybody, but merely because he applies, or rather misapplies, the rules of the system he is learning; but the very misapplication proves that in a sense the child is using the rules.

In foreign language learning the problem of misapplying the rules looms even larger than in the native language. First of all, it is quite likely that in the foreign language you will have less practice—memorize less—than in the native language. The result is that no matter how you study the foreign language, a larger area of what you want to say is left to the application of the rules, and therefore to potential error. But the most essential difference between learning the native language and a foreign language lies in the simple fact that when you learn the foreign language you have already learned (consciously or subconsciously) a set of rules—namely the set that governs the system of the native language. If you learn a foreign language while you are still young, at an age at which the patterns and rules of your native language are still comparatively new to you, the interference that comes from the rules of the native language is likely to be small. But the older you become, the more practice you have had in speaking the native language, the more the rules and system of the native language are likely to interfere with learning the system of the foreign language. Once you are in your teens it is no longer possible to learn the foreign language in exactly the same way in which you learned your native language. The mere fact that you already have a native language that will interfere with the foreign language makes second language learning and first language learning quite different processes.

In no area of language is the interference coming from the native language more obvious than in the sound system. A child learning a foreign language before the age of twelve or thirteen will usually acquire it without accent—but there are very few individuals who will manage to rid themselves of the interference coming from their native sound system if they start the learning of the foreign language after the age of eighteen. The older the person, the more difficult it is to combat the interference coming from the native system, and the more it must be a matter of directed, conscious effort.

Before going into a more detailed discussion of the problem of foreign language learning, let us take a general look at our main enemy, "interference." In the sound system of your native language, you have learned to say certain sounds, and certain sounds only. And that system has sensitized you to hear those sound differences on which its functioning depends. As a native speaker of English you can say the (th) sound of *thin*, and you can hear the difference between this (th) and /s/: obviously *sin* and *thin* are different words; but if your native language has no (th) sound, you might find it extremely difficult to make the sound and—just as important—you might not react to the difference between /s/ and the (th) sound; *sin* and *thin* might sound like the same word.

In the area of vocabulary or word meaning the main problem in foreign language learning is again created by the native language. A word in the foreign language becomes associated with one in the native language and is then reused as if it were the native language word. We can illustrate this kind of foreign language learning accident by an example taken from English alone: Let us assume that by comparing the sentences *I got the book from my friend* and *I received the book from my friend* you come to the conclusion that *got* means *received*. Now apply this equation *got* = *received* to the sentence *I got excited:* you will end up with a meaningless *I received excited*. A word in English does not "mean" another word in English in the sense that it is always substituted for it. The same is also true about the relation of words in different languages, and one of the main temptations that the foreign language learner must avoid is the desire to use a foreign word as if it were the exact counterpart of a word in his own language.

In the area of morphology the foreign language learner is subject to the same temptations as the child just learning his own language. What is more logical than a past tense *readed*, *gived*, etc., all formed on the analogy of *laughed*? To learn that the past tenses involved are *read* and *gave* is—for the native speaker of English as well as for the foreigner—primarily a matter of practice. The main difference is that the native speaker of English got his practice rather painlessly in early childhood by hearing countless instances of correct usage. For the foreigner the practice is likely to take a considerable conscious learning effort.

When it comes to structure, the native language is again likely to cause various types of trouble. First of all, the learner is likely to assemble words according to his native patterns or blueprints rather than those of the foreign language. If in his language pronoun objects are put before the verb, a sentence like *I him see* may look and sound pretty good. Or the learner may change one sentence into another according to the rules of his own language. If in his language a positive sentence is made negative by putting a simple negative before the verb, then it is quite obvious that the negative of *I speak English* is *I not speak English*. Yet another possibility of error is introduced because the foreigner who has learned the rule that tells him how to change one type of sentence to another may not be aware of the limits or exceptions which apply to that rule: as a native speaker of English you know that the rule of using *do* in a negative sentence (*I do not know*, *I do not speak*, etc.) does not apply when you use words like *may*, *must*, *can*, etc. A foreigner may miss this "exception." If that is so, he may tell you that *he does not can understand you so very well*.

3

Learning a

Foreign Language

There are many methods of teaching languages and a considerable amount of controversy as to the best way of teaching foreign languages. For a long time the so-called *grammar-translation method* was prevalent, at least in school situations. The distinguishing features of the grammar-translation approach are (1) insistence upon grammatical analysis and (2) the assumption that grammatical categories can be defined in general terms with reference to meaning. Thus the grammatical categories serve, so to speak, as the common denominator for all languages. According to the grammar-translation method, the best way to say a sentence in a foreign language is to start with a sentence in the native language, analyze it grammatically into such components as *subject* (who performs the action), *verb* (which denotes the action), *object* (which receives the action), etc. If necessary, the categories are then further analyzed: e.g., the person, tense, mood, etc. of the verb are determined. Then the pupil is told to find the corresponding forms in the foreign language. Sounds, morphemes, words are of course always considered peculiar to one language alone, but the patterns of language (the syntax) are thought of as universals that will allow the pupil to go from one language to another. Of course, everybody knows that many patterns of a foreign language do not agree with those of the native language, and those contrasting patterns have to be learned or memorized as "exceptions" (exceptions of one language from the viewpoint of another). Thus a Frenchman learning English would have to learn that in English you say *You obey your father* (you didn't know that this was an exception, did you?), and the speaker of English learning French would have to be taught that for some peculiar reason the French insist on saying **Vous obéissez à votre père** (literally *you obey to your father*).

Opposed to the grammar-translation method are the advocates of the direct approach. The so-called *direct method* is based on the rationale that interference from the native language is the arch-enemy of all language learning and that the foreign language can be learned easily and correctly only if the native language is by-passed altogether in the learning process. Typically, direct-method teachers involve the pupil in conversation and supply meaning by referring directly to objects and picture charts; they act out the meaning of sentences in order to make themselves understood. Some direct-method teachers feel that they can do better without reference to any sort of grammatical analysis; others use grammar. If they use the direct method consistently, then the grammar offered to the student is that of the foreign language alone—the grammar of the native language is not referred to, nor is the native language used in the grammatical explanation.

Another approach that is currently used very widely, especially in secondary school and colleges, is the so-called *audio-lingual method*. Unlike the direct method, the audio-lingual method admits the use of the native language to supply meaning to the student. At the same time it involves a great deal of memorization on the part of the student—especially in the initial stages of instruction. Typically, the material memorized consists of dialogues that the pupil can act out. Reading and writing are not generally used during the initial phases of instruction, because it is thought that these activities might, at least in the beginning, interfere with the development of audio-lingual skills, and that especially the use of writing may lead to spelling pronunciation. The audio-lingual method also shares with the direct method the rejection of translation as a tool, or at least as the main tool, of instruction. The grammatical exercises used in this method usually take the form of drills in which the student is asked to substitute words for other words, or to make changes in sentences (e.g., from singular to plural, from past to present, etc.).

It is not our purpose here to weigh the relative merits of teaching methods. As a matter of fact, a good case could be made for as well as against some aspects of all of them. There are, however, a few important facts that the language learner has to keep in mind. (1) No matter what method is used, language learning requires a great deal of practice and perseverance—ultimately we learn only what we do. It is impossible to learn to understand a language without listening to it a great deal, just as it is impossible to learn to speak a language without speaking it. (2) No matter what method is used, some people seem to be more successful language learners than others. From all the evidence it seems that relative success and failure of an individual in learning a language is not significantly influenced by the teaching method. In other words, good learners have a certain aptitude that poor learners lack, and—more important—good learners do certain things that poor language learners do not do. (3) Whatever the disadvantages of lower language aptitude may be, in no other subject is it more evident that these disadvantages can—in most cases at least—be overcome by sufficient practice. Thus all immigrants coming to the United States eventually learn to speak English—no matter what their educational level or language aptitude—*provided* that they continue to expose themselves with determination and purpose to an English-speaking environment.

Since foreign language learning requires a great deal of practice, it is almost certain that no matter what teaching method is used, the pupil will spend a great deal of time studying by himself, at home with a textbook, or in the laboratory with a tape. In other words, the pupil spends a great deal of time teaching himself. It is for this reason that we shall ask the reader to assume at times the teacher's point of view. In doing so, he will be able to realize that good teaching methods are also essentially good learning methods, and that the successful language learner is essentially the pupil who has (consciously or not) devised a successful self-teaching method.

Before approaching the problem of language learning in some detail, we must ask ourselves again just what is involved in learning a foreign language. We can start by reviewing the general picture of language that we have just outlined.

We described language as a system composed of elements of various levels: small building stones making up larger building stones, which, in turn, must fit into definite construction patterns. Regardless of the specific teaching method, the goal of language learning must be memorization or automatic mastery of all the elements of the lower levels. In other words, speaking a language involves being able to say and distinguish its sounds; it involves knowing the words and the patterns in which the words are arranged. On the higher levels, the "idiomatic expressions" (these are structures that do not have the meaning that one would expect them to have according to their component elements) must, almost by definition, be learned and memorized. In other words, there are levels and elements of language for which memorization and practice alone are the dominant aspects of learning: you cannot use a word if you don't know it; you cannot use (or understand) an idiom if you have not learned it.

It is really only on the higher level—namely that of syntactical patterning—that the question of understanding versus memorization arises. Here the language learner should keep in mind two apparently contradictory facts: (1) the more material (sentences, dialogues, etc.) you memorize, the better; (2) memorization alone cannot solve the problem. In your native language you did not memorize all the possible utterances, but you learned to control a system. Your goal in foreign language learning must be the same.

There are many teaching methods—some of them commercially available on records or tapes—that are advertised as bringing about startling results. Often they are packaged with statements assuring the learner that, if he follows the method, he will be able to speak the foreign language fluently in six weeks to three months. Actually there is no particular trick or deception involved. What the advertising promises is in fact that if you are willing to memorize a certain amount of material you will know it. It is not the *method* that performs the trick, it is the learner. And—to stress again—neither is the memorization of a great deal of material without value. In the area of pronunciation (and especially intonation), correctness and fluency are inevitably linked: you cannot give a correct intonation to a fractured sentence hesitantly produced. Thus fluency through memorization is a necessity in the early stages of any language learning experience. In addition, the more material you know by heart, the more material you will have available for immediate use and the more models you will have to follow and to construct your utterances on.

This brings us to the main point of our discussion. How do you produce your own utterances in the foreign language? Here we can distinguish two basically opposed methods: a wrong one and a right one. The wrong one consists in taking a sentence in your native language as the starting point, looking for foreign language equivalents of the individual words, and putting them together. This method requires a maximum of time and is most likely to produce fractured sentences in the foreign language. The right method consists of looking for a base sentence in the foreign language, using material that you know to be correct as raw material, and converting it into what you want to say.

Let us assume that you want to say in language X: *I am sorry that you didn't understand me*. The wrong way would be to think of the equivalents for *I, sorry, understand*, etc., and then to try to put them together. The right way is to think of a sentence that is part of the stock of sentences available to you—part of the raw material at your disposal. This sentence might be *I am so glad that she will come*. This sentence can be converted into what you want to say by a few substitutions (*sorry* for *glad, you* for *she, understand* for *come*), and grammatical changes (e.g., change in the tense of the verb). The process involved will be the easier and the more rapid the closer the base sentence is to the sentence that is the goal of the operation. The correct formation of the sentence will still require an understanding of the grammar of the foreign language. In other words, you have to know what words can be substituted for each other and how sentence structures can be changed. However, as you go on learning the foreign language you will find that you learn more and more sentences that become models for what you want to say, so that the area of substituting and changing is steadily narrowed down. At the same time you also get practice in performing the processes of changing and substituting more rapidly. Finally, when the available number of models is very large, and when your ability to change and substitute has increased to the point where you perform the processes almost subconsciously and with great rapidity, then you may say that you are approaching the fluency and control of the native speaker.

One more bit of general advice: As we have just stated, your fluency in the language depends to a very large degree on the model utterance that you may be able to think of in a specific situation. Sentences or utterances that you have learned in connection with a specific situation are likely to suggest themselves again as models if you are in a similar situation. Sentences and utterances learned *without being associated with anything* are not likely to occur to you again. It is thus quite helpful and important to *learn to associate utterances with situations.* If the textbook you happen to be using follows an approach that connects sentences with specific situations, you have only to follow the book. If the book does not provide the situational tie-in, *you can do it yourself.* In other words, with every sentence you are asked to produce, translate, repeat, etc., you should *try to use your imagination to think up very quickly a situation in which this sentence might have been used.* Even such maligned theoretical "grammar book sentences" as *My aunt's pen is not in the garden* are not useless, provided that you learn them as sentences that could have been said in a specific situation, and that you know how to incorporate them into your stock of usable "raw material."

The opposite side of the coin is of course to get into the habit of thinking of possible foreign language utterances in situations in which you might find yourself. To tell you to go to the foreign country and to place yourself in a situation where you continuously hear and are forced to use the foreign language is cheap advice that may be expensive to follow; but once you have had a few months of classroom contact with the foreign language, you can try the following experiment: At least three times daily, *imagine* that you are in the foreign country and will have to respond in the foreign language. Pick different situations every day—getting in the streetcar, buying groceries, getting gas at a filling station, etc. If you feel that your response might have been inadequate, go back to your textbook (or your teacher—hopefully he will be cooperative), find out how your response could have been improved, and try again.

One final word: Let us stress again that our advice concerns a method of learning, not a method of teaching. The prerequisite for following the advice consists of having available a stock of model sentences and some understanding of the grammatical structure of the foreign language—enough understanding to be able to execute the conversion processes. Whether these prerequisites are provided by a grammar-translation method. a direct method, or an audio-lingual "linguistic" method is *not* of primary relevance. There is of course a certain agreement between the audio-lingual linguistic teaching method and our description of correct language learning. But then again we are talking about performance by the pupil, not by the teacher. In our context, changing sentences or substituting in them are not ways by which the pupil is manipulated into the repetition of utterances, but devices used by the learner to achieve the goal of self-expression in the foreign language.

II

The Nature of Language

4

The Sounds

of English

A. THE CONSONANTS OF ENGLISH

We have stated in the previous chapter that the human voice is capable of producing a great variety of sounds that are potential speech sounds. The science of *phonetics* deals with the description of these sounds, either by analyzing their acoustical properties or by studying the precise method of their production. To understand just how speech sounds are produced is of course important for the student of language. Speech sounds of foreign languages are sometimes quite similar to those of English, but often they are quite different. In any event, it is helpful to know just how the sounds of English are produced so that we can learn just how those of the foreign language differ, how we must modify the English sound in order to produce the foreign sound. It is for this reason that we start our discussion with a description of the production of the significant sounds of English.

Speech sounds are usually classified into the broad categories of vowels and consonants. *Vowels* are the sounds in the production of which the airstream is allowed to go through the speech organs without meeting any obstacle. The *consonants* are the sounds produced by the creation of an obstacle that impedes the progress of the airstream through the speech tracts. The most important way of classifying the consonants is thus to group them according to the place at which the obstacle is produced. Other ways of classification include the exact nature of the obstacle and the so-called difference in voicing. Voiced consonants (for example, the *b* of *bit*) are produced with a simultaneous vibration of the vocal cords, while voiceless consonants (the *p* of *pit*) are produced without that vibration. As far as the exact nature of the obstacle is concerned, the main difference lies between the so-called *stops* and the *continuants*. In the case of the stops, the obstacle actually stops the airstream completely, and the sound is produced by the noise made by the sudden release (for example, the *p* of *pin*). With continuant sounds the obstacle is never complete; the sound is produced by the airstream going through a narrowed passage (e.g., the passage left between the lower lip and upper teeth during the production of *f* as in *fin*).

For the time being, however, we shall concentrate on the place of production alone and look at the consonants of English from that point of view. In discussing the sounds, we shall introduce some technical terminology and some symbols to denote the sounds. The symbols are necessary because the *orthography* (spelling or way of writing) of English—like that of many other languages—is often ambiguous and confusing; the same sound is frequently represented by different symbols or the same symbols used to represent different sounds. Thus in the discussion of sounds it is customary to use a special alphabet in which each sound is represented by only one symbol. In reading the following discussion of the sounds, it will be helpful actually to pronounce the sounds and sample words and to check the diagram of the speech organs. We shall begin with the point of articulation at the front of the speech tract and work our way back.

1. Sounds produced by both lips (4, 4): *Bilabials*

/p/ as in Pin, Pine, sPin, sPot, cuP, hiccouGH

In our examples we shall write the orthographic symbols corresponding to the sound in capital letters. In our examples we can note two important facts: (1) The orthography is of course not always consistent; note that /p/ in hiccough is spelled *gh*. (2) We have already noted that the /p/ of *pin* is really not the same as the /p/ of *spin*. Since we are discussing the significant sounds (phonemes) of English, we can overlook this

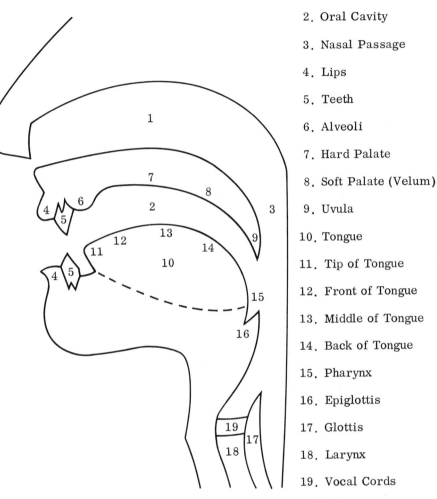

1. Nasal Cavity
2. Oral Cavity
3. Nasal Passage
4. Lips
5. Teeth
6. Alveoli
7. Hard Palate
8. Soft Palate (Velum)
9. Uvula
10. Tongue
11. Tip of Tongue
12. Front of Tongue
13. Middle of Tongue
14. Back of Tongue
15. Pharynx
16. Epiglottis
17. Glottis
18. Larynx
19. Vocal Cords

difference here, just as—from the point of view of English alone—we can overlook the fact that the /p/ of *cup* is still different from the /p/ of either *pin* or *spin*. If you watch your pronunciation carefully, you will probably notice that the /p/ of *cup* does not have the same full "explosion" of the airstream as that of *pin*.

/b/ as in Buy, Boom, Bin, laBoratory, taB
/m/ as in May, Mother, booM
/w/ as in Water, Win, alWays

2. Sounds produced with upper teeth and lower lip
   (5, 4): *Labiodentals*

   /f/ as in Fine, Father, lauGH, PHoneme
   /v/ as in Vain, loVe

3. Sounds produced with the tip of the tongue against
   the teeth (11, 5): *Dentals*

   /θ/ as in THin, THink, breaTH
   /ð/ as in THat, THose, breaTHe, THese

4. Sounds produced with the tip of the tongue against
   the gums of the upper teeth (the little grooves
   behind the teeth that you can feel with the tip of
   the tongue are called the *alveoli*) (11, 6): *Alveolars*

   /t/ as in Tin, sTay, cuT

   Note that the three /t/ sounds above are different from each other in the
   same ways in which the /p/'s of *pin*, *spin*, and *cup* are different. The /t/
   of *stay* is unaspirated (not followed by a small puff of air), and the /t/ of
   cut is typically unreleased.

   /d/ as in Den, haD, laDDer
   /l/ as in Late, biLL, caLLer
   /n/ as in Not, siN, wiNNer
   /s/ as in Sing, graSS, Ceiling
   /z/ as in Zinc, waS, roSe

   Note that in the production of the last two sounds there is a slight groove
   formed in the front of the tongue. It is actually this groove, rather than
   the tip of the tongue, that is against the alveoli.

5. Sounds produced with the tip of the tongue curled
   back toward the palate (11, 7): *Retroflex*

   This is characteristic of the production of the /r/ sound used by many
   Americans in words like *peaRl*, *Red*, etc.

6. Sounds produced with the front of the tongue (not
   the very tip) against the gums of the upper teeth
   (12, 6): *Alveopalatals*

/č/ as in CHin, CHurCH, reaCH, caTCH
/ǰ/ as in General, Gin, riDGE, Jam, JuDGE
/ʃ/ as in SHip, waSH, preSSure, fiSSion, naTIon
/ʒ/ as in treaSure, viSIon, beiGE

7. Sounds produced with the middle of the tongue against the front of the palate (13, 7): *Prepalatal*

/y/ as in Yes, Yet

8. Sounds produced with the back of the tongue against the back of the palate (14, 7): *Palatals*

/k/ as in Kin, sKin

Note that just like the /p/ in *spin*, the /k/ in *skin* is unaspirated, while the /k/ in *kin* is aspirated.

/g/ as in Gimmick, GUild, Get, diG
/ŋ/ as in siNG, cliNG

9. Sounds produced with the back of the tongue against the soft palate, the so-called *velum* (14, 8): *Velars*

/k/ as in Caught, Cot, Could, booK, sCHool, blaCK

Note that the /k/ sounds in *kin* and *could* are thus not really the same; the difference, however, is again the one between two variants (*allophones*) of the same phoneme as far as English is concerned. Since the vowel of *kin* is farther forward than the vowel of *could*, the consonant preceding it is also produced farther forward.

/g/ as in Go, GHoul, ruG

Note here again that the /g/ of *go* is not really the same as that of *get*. The difference depends again on the following vowel and is thus—as far as English is concerned—just the difference between two variants (allophones) of the same sound.

/ŋ/ as in baNG, soNG

Note again that in English the difference between /ŋ/ in *sing* and /ŋ/ in *song* is only a distinction between variants of one phoneme.

10. Sounds produced in the glottis by the vocal cords
     (17, 19): *Glottals*

/ʔ/ If the vocal cords are closed, they impede the airstream that comes up against them. If the cords are suddenly opened, a stop sound is produced. This stop sound /ʔ/ cannot be described as a significant sound of English, but it is produced by some speakers of American English (New Yorkers, New Jerseyites) as a variation of the /t/ phoneme in words like *boTTle*.

/h/ as in Have, WHo, Hill

This sound is produced by the friction of the air passing through the constriction created by the vocal cords.

After reviewing the principal points of production or articulation used for English consonants, we can briefly note the different manners of production involved in the consonants discussed: /p/, /t/, /k/ and their voiced counterparts /b/, /d/, /g/ are—as we have mentioned already—stop sounds. The airstream is interrupted completely by the obstacle and then released very suddenly, and the sound that is thus produced is somewhat reminiscent of the noise created by a sudden explosion (an alternate name for the stop sounds is *plosives*). The sounds /č/ (*CHin*) and its voiced counterpart /ǰ/ (*Gin*) are also stops, but they are stops produced with a very slow release. The effect of the slow release is that these sounds can in fact be considered as made up of two sounds: a stop and then a continuant sound produced at the same point of articulation.

The sounds /m/ (*Mat*), /n/ (*No*), and /ŋ/ (*siNG*) are *nasals*. They are stop sounds insofar as the airstream is completely interrupted at their point of articulation in the oral air passage, but the velum is flapped down so that the air can escape through the nasal passage and the nasal cavity. One might say that all of these sounds—which in English are always voiced—are oral stops and nasal continuants.

The rest of the consonants discussed so far are all continuants. Their production does not involve any complete stoppage of the airstream at any one time. Most of them are *fricatives*. This means that they are produced through the friction that the airstream creates as it is forced through the obstacles during the production of the sound. In the case of the sounds /h/, /f/, /θ/ and the voiced counterparts of the latter two, /v/, /ð/, the air goes through an obstacle resembling a narrow slit opening. They are called *slit fricatives*. With the sounds /s/, /ʃ/ and their voiced counterparts /z/, /ʒ/, the production of the sound is modified by the tongue forming a groove. You can note this grooving by comparing your pronunciation of *thin* (tongue flat) with that of *sin* (note the groove?). The grooving of the tongue gives the sounds a hissing quality, and thus /s/, /z/, /ʃ/, /ʒ/ are called *sibilants* or *groove fricatives*.

The sounds /w/, /r/, /y/ are often classified as *semivowels*. Since their production does not involve any friction noise and the air passage is relatively free, they come close to the quality of vowels. You should especially note that the /r/ of English is really very much like a vowel. It can be prolonged, there is no friction noise, there is no contact between the tongue and the alveolar ridge. Also in a somewhat special category is the sound /l/. Since during its production the airstream is allowed to pass on both sides of the tongue, it is generally called a *lateral* (**latus** in Latin means side). In our discussion we have classified it as an alveolar from the point of view of point of articulation. Many speakers of English do produce the /l/ with the tip of the tongue against the gums of the upper teeth. However, you may also find that you produce /l/—generally before other consonants, in words like *milk*—by drawing the tongue back against the velum without the tip of the tongue even coming close to the gums of the upper teeth.

We can thus summarize our discussion of consonant sounds as illustrated by English in the accompanying chart. As you look at it you will notice (1) that English does not take advantage of all the possible points of production (e.g., we did not describe any sound that involves the use of the uvula—see point 9 on the chart of the speech organs); (2) that with all of the points of production that are utilized, you will find empty spaces on your chart. Some of these are of course used by foreign languages that you may know or that you may study. To be able to place these foreign sounds on the chart and to realize their point of articulation may turn out to be a great help in mastering their correct pronunciation.

Manner of Articulation

Points of Articulation	Stops Voiced	Stops Unvcd	Affricates Voiced	Affricates Unvcd	Fricatives Slit Voiced	Fricatives Slit Unvcd	Fricatives Groove Voiced	Fricatives Groove Unvcd	Nasals	Laterals	Semivowels
Bilabial (4, 4)	b (bin)	p (pin)							m (man)		w (water)
Labiodental (4, 5)					v (vat)	f (fat)					
Dental (11, 5)					ð (that)	θ (thin)					
Alveolar (11, 6)	d (din)	t (tin)					z (zinc)	s (sit)	n (no)	l (late)	
Retroflex (11, 7)											r (red)
Alveopalatal (12, 6)			ǰ (gin)	č (chin)			ʒ (vision)	ʃ (she)			
Prepalatal (12, 7)											y (yes)
Palatal (14, 7)	g (get)	k (kin)									
Velar (14, 8)	g (good)	k (could)							ŋ (sing)		
Glottal (19)	ʔ (bottle)					h (hat)					

28

Learning Exercises

In all exercises be sure actually to *pronounce* the words *out loud*. (Do not let the orthography mislead you.)

1. Decide for each pair of words whether they *end* in consonant sounds that both have the same point of articulation, or have final consonants with different points of articulation:

1. cough, dove	5. benign, sing	9. clique, sink
2. was, can	6. damn, bomb	10. rash, badge
3. church, judge	7. state, lead	11. hiss, rage
4. rage, rug	8. fence, fetch	12. felt, stern

   Answer: 1. same 2. same 3. same 4. different 5. different 6. same 7. same 8. different 9. same 10. same 11. different 12. same

2. In the following groups of words, which (if any) has a beginning consonant sound that does not have the same point of articulation as the beginning consonant sounds of the other three?

1. joke, jab, get, gentle	6. fat, van, photo, psalm
2. thin, this, thought, thick	7. know, ken, kid, key
3. gentleman, cherry, shave, sink	8. zebra, silent, psychology, chin
4. ceiling, seat, rate, zero	9. who, whose, whom, white
5. job, chap, gym, gentile	10. chip, zinc, Jim, German

   Answer: 1. get 2. (none) 3. sink 4. rate 5. (none) 6. psalm 7. know 8. chin 9. white 10. zinc

3. In the following groups, which word (if any) ends in a consonant sound that has a different point of articulation than the final consonant sounds of the other words in the same group?

1. watch, rash, garage, rag	3. has, grass, sing, tease
2. bang, gag, kick, sign	4. teeth, bath, thought, breathe

5. cough, rough, hiccough,   8. ring, align, cling, wing
   bluff   9. ban, ball, bad, bath
6. judge, watch, jug, much   10. have, enough, hymn,
7. bomb, rum, come, lip   cliff

Answer: 1. rag 2. sign 3. sing 4. thought 5. hiccough
6. jug 7. (none) 8. align 9. bath 10. hymn

4. In each of the following words, decide whether the final consonant sound has the same point of articulation as the first consonant sound:

1. boom	6. mop	11. teeth
2. lead	7. nod	12. dash
3. loathe	8. cage	13. shine
4. king	9. rage	14. gang
5. gage	10. nothing	15. thought

Answer: 1. yes 2. yes 3. no 4. yes 5. no 6. yes
7. yes 8. no 9. no 10. no 11. no 12. no 13. no
14. yes 15. no

5. Read the following groups of words aloud, paying particular attention to the pronunciation of the initial consonant sound of each word. Notice that the point of articulation of the initial consonant sound of each word in the series is farther back than that of the initial consonant sound of the preceding word.

1. pin, father, that, German, hit
2. bud, that, rough, chin, come, have
3. mood, van, ceiling, jam, yes, can
4. bottle, thistle, new, judge, king, hear
5. wind, philanthropy, certain, right, chin, can, who
6. mother, father, same, yet, kid, could

Now read the series that follow and decide whether the points of articulation of the initial consonants are successively farther back, as in the series you have just practiced:

1. bird, fan, there, know, give
2. my, voice, tongue, gym, clear, hat

3. very, dog, come, chair, man, this
4. pear, three, nose, sugar, girl

Answer: 1. yes   2. yes   3. no   4. yes

6. Read the following groups of words aloud, paying particular attention to the final consonant sound of each word. Notice that the point of articulation of the final consonant sound of each word in the series is farther forward than the point of articulation of the final consonant of the preceding word.

   1. sang, war, geese, tooth, rough, gap
   2. rug, judge, ball, wrath, have, autumn
   3. rag, rash, bat, bath, love
   4. clique, church, sign, wax, cough, balm
   5. sang, sick, fresh, good, warm
   6. gag, rouge, was, enough, hymn

   Now read the series that follow and decide whether the points of articulation of the final consonants are successively farther forward, as in the series you have just practiced:

   1. big, rich, fun, cloth, some
   2. rack, fudge, bit, save, tub
   3. long, wish, load, breathe, laugh
   4. quick, ridge, long, rib, wave

   Answer: 1. yes   2. yes   3. yes   4. no

7. For each of the following pairs, decide whether or not the beginning consonant sounds of the two words differ *only* in their manner of articulation (point of articulation and voicing must be the same):

1. tin, thin	5. giant, church	8. game, gin
2. could, goal	6. zinc, sing	9. dime, late
3. chin, shine	7. never, deer	10. can, have
4. philosophy, pin		

   Answer: 1. no   2. no   3. yes   4. no   5. no   6. no   7. yes
   8. no   9. yes   10. no

8. In each of the following words, is the *second* consonant sound produced in exactly the same manner of articulation as the first?

1. pit   4. size   7. mink   10. teeth
2. judge   5. bitter   8. faith   11. bag
3. heather   6. scissors   9. hoof   12. cob

Answer: 1. yes 2. yes 3. yes 4. yes 5. yes 6. yes
7. yes 8. yes 9. yes 10. no 11. yes 12. yes

9. In each of the following series of words, which word (if any)
   begins with a consonant sound produced in a manner of
   articulation different from that of the initial consonant
   sounds of the other words in the series?

   1. phoneme, van, fine, father
   2. hat, thin, vale, fat
   3. then, thin, home, chin
   4. sin, shine, ceiling, gin
   5. circus, zip, job, shot

   Answer: 1. (none) 2. (none) 3. chin 4. gin 5. job

10. In each of the following series, which word (if any) ends in a
    consonant sound produced in a manner of articulation dif-
    ferent from that of the final consonant sounds of the other
    words in the series?

    1. breathe, enough, brave, both
    2. wash, judge, rouge, cuss
    3. balm, sign, can, malign
    4. knob, claque, kick, warmth
    5. feet, feed, teeth, hip

    Answer: 1. (none) 2. judge 3. (none) 4. warmth 5.
    teeth

11. Which of the following pairs have initial consonant sounds
    differing only by being voiced or unvoiced?

    1. chap, jug   5. than, thunder   8. thought, taught
    2. chin, yoke   6. germ, shine   9. philosophy, van
    3. get, cap   7. pat, mouth   10. ceiling, zeal
    4. foot, vat

    Answer: 1. yes 2. no 3. yes 4. yes 5. yes 6. no
    7. no 8. no 9. yes 10. yes

12. Decide whether or not the following pairs have final consonant sounds differing only by being voiced or unvoiced.

    1. has, grass   5. rug, ridge   8. good, catch
    2. wash, watch   6. wash, rouge   9. index, rose
    3. knife, laugh   7. cough, wave   10. sneeze, nice
    4. had, hate

    Answer: 1. yes 2. no 3. no 4. yes 5. no 6. yes 7. yes
    8. no 9. yes 10. yes

13. For each of the following words, write out the *phonetic symbol* representing the sound of the letter or letters written in capitals in the orthographic representation of the word (check with the chart of symbols if necessary).

    1. siNG   6. caTCH   11. beTTer
    2. THose   7. enouGH   12. buZZes
    3. haS   8. riDGE   13. piLLs
    4. thouGHT   9. couLD   14. pillS
    5. WHom   10. miSSion   15. pleaSure

    Answer: 1. ŋ 2. ð 3. z 4. t 5. h 6. č 7. f 8. ǰ
    9. d 10. ʃ 11. t 12. z 13. l 14. z 15. ʒ

14. This exercise should be tried only with the supervision of an instructor.

    1. Try to make continuant sounds produced at the same point of articulation as /p/, /b/. Say *pa, ba*; then shift to a continuant sound by slowly releasing the obstacle created by the lips.
    2. Try to say *ta, da, la, na* by producing *t, d, l, n* as *dentals* rather than alveolars (tip of the tongue against the *teeth*, not the *alveolae*).
    3. Try to make an affricate out of *p, t* by releasing the obstacle to the air stream very slowly.
    4. Try to produce continuant sounds at the position of /k/, /g/. Say *ka, ga*. Then release the obstacle very gradually.
    5. Try to produce the sound /ŋ/ (siNG) as the beginning of a syllable: say /ŋa/, /ŋo/. You will find it rather difficult.

B. THE VOWELS OF ENGLISH

The production of the vowel sounds does not involve the creation of any definite obstacle to the airstream. What differentiates vowels from each other are various modifications of the *resonator* (oral and nasal cavities) brought about by changes in the position of the tongue and the lips. In producing the vowel sound of English *beat*, the tongue is raised high toward the front of the oral cavity. Thus we classify the vowel of *beat* as a "high front vowel." In the pronunciation of the vowel sound of *boot*, the tongue is still high, but raised toward the back of the mouth. The vowel of *boot* is a "high back vowel." In the production of *beat* the lips are spread, while in *boot* they are rounded. Thus the vowel of *beat* is classified as "unrounded," as opposed to that of *boot*, which is "rounded."

In the following classification of the vowel sounds of American English we must keep in mind (1) that the entire scheme has been somewhat simplified, and (2) that the pronunciation of vowels varies considerably according to region. Another problem concerning the vowels of English arises because many of them are *diphthongal*. This means that during their production the tongue does not stay in the same position, but glides either up or down. The effect of this gliding of the tongue is of course that the vowel is in fact made up of two vowel sounds produced in the same airstream. If the two vowels that make up the diphthong are quite different from each other, it is obvious that we are dealing with two sounds. This is the case with the diphthongs /au/ as in *hOUse, fOWl*; /aɪ/ as in *tIE, bUY, fIle*; and /ɔɪ/ as in *bOY, fOIl*. Actually the vowels in *beat* or *food* or *bone* are also diphthongal, and some linguists have proposed to interpret them as diphthongs. If we do this, the entire phonemic interpretation of the English vowel system changes: a word like *beat* is then interpreted as /bɪyt/ rather than /bit/. For various reasons—primarily for simplicity—we have chosen *not* to follow this interpretation, but we *do* insist on the basically diphthongal quality of the vowels whenever it is present.

The vowel phonemes of English are, then, the following:

1. Front vowels

   /i/ as in bEAt, kEY, recEIve, pEOple
   /ɪ/ as in bIt, pIt, gYm
   /e/ as in bAIt, grEAt, plAY, rEIn
   /ɛ/ as in bEt, vEssel
   /æ/ as in bAt, lAtter

   Note that English uses various orthographic symbols to represent especially the vowels /i/ and /e/. Note also that /i/ and /e/ are highly
   diphthongal. In other words, during their production the tongue glides
   upward in the mouth so that they end with a much higher sound than
   the one with which they begin.

2. Central vowels

   /ə/ as in cUt, pUtt, enOUgh, thUnder, fUr, About, sofA

   Note that this particular vowel occurs in a fairly large variety of forms.
   The pronunciation before /r/ (*fur*) is quite different from that before
   other consonants (e.g., *bun, suds*). Still another variant is the very frequent occurrence of this vowel sound in unstressed position (compare
   the pronunciation of the first and third vowel with that of the second
   in *cOnsUltAnt*). Since, however, these differences are never utilized to
   distinguish words from each other, we can say that so far as English is
   concerned, all the different pronunciations of /ə/ (e.g., *bUt, EnOUgh,
   cOnsUltAnt*) are variants of the same sound unit.

   /a/ as in fAther, pOt, bOttle, sOck, hOt

   Note that for some parts of the United States the above examples (with
   the exception of *father*) may not fit. In some areas, New England, for
   example, words like *hot, pot*, etc., are pronounced somewhat differently.

3. Back vowels

   /u/ as in fOOd, sOUp, nEWs, canOE
   /ʊ/ as in gOOd, cOUld, pUt
   /o/ as in bOAt, sOUl, sEW, slOW, flOE, brOOch
   /ɔ/ as in bOUght, tAUght, lAW, clOth, tAlk

   With the above vowels note again the variety of possible orthographic
   representations, of which we are giving only a sample, and the fact that

especially /u/ (*food*) and /o/ (*boat*) are highly diphthongal. Both sounds end with the tongue in a higher position and with more lip rounding than that with which they began.

Generally we can also note that the front vowels of English are produced with spread lips, and the back vowels with rounded lips. In the case of the central vowels, the lip position may be said to be neutral. There is of course no reason to assume that this state of affairs cannot be different with languages other than English. In studying foreign languages, you may already have learned (or you may have to learn) how to say front vowels with rounded lips, or back vowels with spread lips. This may cause some difficulty, but it does not usually represent an insurmountable problem.

Learning Exercises

1. In each of the following series, which word (if any) does not contain the same stressed vowel sound as the rest of the words in the series?

   1. great, brain, said, say
   2. boat, sew, flow, towel
   3. chute, food, moon, soup
   4. toll, goat, raccoon, flow
   5. bread, bed, pleasure, ten
   6. tray, great, vain, bead
   7. fate, may, rein, key
   8. put, book, food, would
   9. good, could, but, put
   10. pot, cot, bone, chop
   11. meet, receive, seat, complete
   12. meat, people, seat, believe
   13. bought, soup, caught, thought
   14. gate, stay, thank, hail
   15. blew, toe, canoe, soon
   16. house, towel, plow, tow
   17. straight, gauge, play, cane
   18. flea, amoeba, seed, weasel
   19. buy, tie, train, aisle
   20. ghoul, goal, stone, foe

   Answer: 1. said 2. towel 3. (none) 4. raccoon 5. (none) 6. bead 7. key 8. food 9. but 10. bone 11. (none) 12. (none) 13. soup 14. thank 15. toe 16. tow 17. (none) 18. (none) 19. train 20. ghoul

2. Pronounce the following words and observe the pronunciation of the stressed vowel sounds. Decide whether the vowel sound

is pronounced with spread lips, with rounded lips, or with lips neither spread nor rounded:

1. bitter   2. stay   3. stew   4. peat   5. gift
6. coat   7. duck   8. toe   9. tea   10. fill

Answer: 1. spread   2. spread   3. rounded   4. spread   5. spread   6. rounded   7. neither   8. rounded   9. spread   10. spread

3. We have stated that many English vowel phonemes are diphthongal. Pronounce the following words and observe the pronunciation of the vowel sound. Notice whether during the pronunciation of the vowel sound the tongue glides up and *forward*, up and *backward* accompanied by lip-rounding, or makes *neither* of these glide movements:

1. tote	7. stood	13. leave
2. ship	8. blood	14. loose
3. boat	9. float	15. go
4. few	10. quay	16. caught
5. stole	11. should	17. day
6. flew	12. rope	18. key

Answer: These may vary somewhat with individual pronunciation. Most likely the answers should be:

1. backward   2. neither   3. backward   4. backward   5. backward   6. backward   7. neither   8. neither   9. backward   10. forward   11. neither   12. backward   13. forward   14. backward   15. backward   16. neither   17. forward   18. forward

4. For each of the following words write the symbol of the vowel phoneme which corresponds to the orthographic symbols written in capital letters:

1. cAUght	6. rOUgh	11. OAk
2. sIng	7. stEAdy	12. rAIn
3. lAter	8. mOOn	13. dAY
4. bOOk	9. bUY	14. sOUp
5. blOOd	10. stOne	15. fOUl

Answer: 1. ɔ   2. ɪ   3. e   4. ʊ   5. ə   6. ə   7. ɛ   8. u   9. aɪ   10. o   11. o   12. e   13. e   14. u   15. aʊ

5. Do this exercise only with the supervision of the teacher.

    1. Say the vowel /i/ (bEAt). Then, while holding the tongue position constant, try to say the vowel while rounding your lips. (Start by saying /i/ and then round your lips as you continue to produce the vowel sound.)

    2. Say the vowel /u/ (fOOd). Then try to spread your lips while continuing to say the vowel sound, so that you produce the /u/ vowel with unrounded lips.

    3. Try to say the vowels /i/ (bEAt) and /u/ (fOOd) without glides. You may try to say the vowel and keep your tongue from gliding up, or you may try to pronounce the vowel normally. Let your tongue glide up, and then say a vowel keeping the tongue in the higher position reached at the end of the English /i/ or /u/.

C. STRESS AND INTONATION PATTERNS OF ENGLISH

The intonation patterns of a language often represent one of the most difficult learning problems. Individuals who have achieved great fluency and accuracy in a foreign language often retain the characteristic intonations and stresses of their native language. It is for this reason that we shall pay some attention to an understanding of the intonation and stress patterns of English as an example of one type of stress and intonation system. The most important feature to realize about intonation and stresses is that they are not merely haphazard "melodies" superimposed upon the language, but part and parcel of the signaling system, of the "code" of the language itself.

We have already made the point that in English the stress or absence of stress on a syllable makes a difference. We have mentioned the difference between *pérmit* (noun) and *permít* (verb), which is produced by a change in stress. We could add examples like *áddress, addréss; rébel, rebél; díscus, discúss* in which the presence of a heavy stress or its absence makes a difference in meaning. Yet in addition to a heavy stress (usually transcribed as ′) and absence of stress (usual transcription ˘), English has two more degrees of stress that seem to make a difference in the meaning of an utterance. Thus, if you compare your pronunciation of the adjective *animate* (as in the expression *animate object*) with that of the verb *animate* (to *animate* the conversation), you will notice a difference in the degree of stress given to the pronunciation of the third syllable. In the adjective, the last syllable is unstressed. In the verb, it has a stress that is stronger than the unstressed second syllable, but less strong than the heavy, or primary, stress on the first syllable. This stress is usually classified as tertiary stress (transcribed `): thus, *ánĭmăte* (adjective) versus *ánĭmàte* (verb).

What we have said above implies that there still remains a secondary stress to be discussed. This can be isolated if we look at sentences like: *Mr. Redman is not really a red man* (heavy stress on *red*), or *This blackbird is really a black bird* (heavy stress on *black*). In such sentences a stress pattern '` (*Rédmàn, bláckbìrd*) seems distinct from a pattern in which the second syllable seems slightly more stressed. This degree of stress is classified as secondary stress (transcription ^), and we can thus contrast in the sentences above a stress '` (*Rédmàn, bláckbìrd*) with a stress pattern '^ (*réd mân, bláck bîrd*).

The above examples introduce yet another important feature of English intonation. In *Redman* or *blackbird* the two words or syllables seem closely linked with each other; at least they would be in normal pronunciation. But in the pronunciation *bláck bîrd* or *réd mân* you will notice a pause or some sort of separation between the two words. This pause (transcribed +) is an important feature of English pronunciation and is used to indicate how syllables or words may be connected and interpreted in the sentence. You can hear the effects of this open transition if you compare your pronunciation of *nitrate* with that of *night + rate* or *ice cream* with *I + scream*. (Note that this open transition can be expressed in different ways: In *night rate* it is expressed by an unreleased pronunciation of the *t* of *night*, which distinguishes the final *t* of night from the first *t* of *nitrate*, which is fully exploded.) To the native speaker of English this open transition is a big help in analyzing and comprehending the stream of speech. (Remember that a foreign language may not give you the same kind of help.)

In addition to stresses and transitions, English has one more tool that helps to communicate meaning as part of intonation and intonation pattern. This is the pitch, or rather the differences in pitch on which various syllables can be pronounced. Since pitch corresponds to the concept of how high or low one's voice is, we can think of it in terms of musical notation. Most linguists think that English differentiates four levels of pitch. If you watch your intonation in making a statement like *I went to the movies* you will note that your pitch seems to go along fairly evenly until the word *movies*. Then it takes a sudden turn upward and on the last syllable of the word makes a sharp drop. Thus your intonation of *I went to the movies* can be notated as:

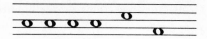

or by means of a so-called intonation contour as:

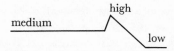

The intonation pattern starts on the *medium* level, goes to *high*, and finishes on *low*. Most English sentences show an alternation of these three levels of pitch. An *extra high level* is sometimes used if the voice expresses emotions like excitement, fear, incredulity, etc. Thus you might say as a matter-of-fact statement: *He has a headache* (*medium—high—low*):

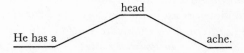

But the same words uttered as an expression of questioning or dismay might become:

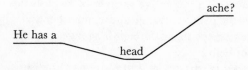

(*medium—low—extra high*).

In addition to the pitch pattern, the way in which the very end of a word standing before a pause is pronounced carries slight variation in meaning. Normally, if you make a simple statement (*I have a headache*) your voice fades out at the end of the statement and the volume of the voice diminishes rapidly (*fading clause terminal*). If you say the same sentence but sustain the pitch at the end of *headache* and prolong the last syllable (*sustained clause terminal*), you indicate to your listener that you are not really finished with your statement; Some additional statement, probably beginning with *yet* or *but*, is about to come. Finally, in the above-quoted *He has a headache?* question of surprise or dismay, your voice rose sharply in pitch toward the end, and the volume did not diminish gradually, but was cut off sharply (*rising clause terminal*).

The purpose of this discussion of English intonation is not, of course, to give an exhaustive picture of the linguistic analysis of this part of the system of the English language; but it is important for us to realize the importance of intonation in language and to emphasize again the fact that its stress and pitch patterns are peculiar to a particular language. Of all the parts of language, intonation and stress are the ones that we take most for granted, that seem most "natural" to us; but let us remember that the intonation patterns that we have just described are the patterns of English. As foreign language students we ought to know them in order to avoid using them in languages other than English. For the intonation patterns of English, if superimposed upon another language, are likely to create damage to communication, which may be anywhere from slight to irreparable.

Learning Exercises

1. Copy the following words on a piece of paper and indicate the syllable bearing the primary stress with the appropriate symbol.

   1. going
   2. nationality
   3. wine cellar
   4. protest (verb)
   5. principle
   6. adhere
   7. clothing store
   8. homework
   9. definition
   10. Frenchman

11. French teacher (one   12. French teacher (one who
    who teaches French)   is born in France)

Answer: 1. góing   2. nationálity   3. wíne cellar   4. protést   5. prínciple   6. adhére   7. clóthing store   8. hómework   9. definítion   10. Frénchman   11. Frénch teacher   12. French téacher

2. Copy the following sentences on a piece of paper and write the appropriate symbols for the stresses and transitions that distinguish the pronunciation of the *italicized* parts.

  1. The *White House* is really a *white house*.
  2. This *bearskin* tickles my *bare skin*.
  3. The *Spitfire* (airplane) began to *spit fire* at the enemy.
  4. Let's *play house* in our *playhouse*.
  5. The *orderly-room* was not a very *orderly room*.
  6. The *whitefish* is not really a *white fish* (stress on white).
  7. I didn't find any *redwood* in *Redwood City*.
  8. He began to *elaborate* on his rather *elaborate* ideas.

Answer: 1. Whíte Hoùse, whìte hoúse (possibly whíte hoúse)   2. béarskìn, bàre skín (possibly bâre skín)   3. Spítfìre, spît + fíre   4. plây + hoúse, pláyhoùse   5. órdĕrlў + roôm, ôrdĕrly + roóm   6. whítefìsh, whíte + fîsh   7. rédwoòd, Rêdwoòd + Cíty   8. ĕlábŏràte, ĕlábŏrăte

3. Indicate the number of phonemes in each of the following words.

  1. quickly   5. hiccough   9. youth
  2. merrily   6. grass   10. phoneme
  3. separate   7. doubt   11. ration
  4. chicken   8. whose   12. revision

Answer: 1. six   2. six   3. seven   4. five   5. five   6. four   7. four   8. three   9. three   10. five   11. five   12. seven

4. In the following series of words, decide which (if any) is made up of a different number of phonemes from the other words in the same group.

  1. stood, bought, put   3. still, girl, thought
  2. cute, mate, rain   4. gallop, bolt, claim

5. caught, sail, tool	11. cleaning, friendly, plainly
6. ready, desk, called	12. onion, scout, style
7. tongue, steep, town	13. quake, daily, thumb
8. belly, through, lady	14. catchy, cart, bought
9. eight, seek, bomb	15. enough, autumn, knob
10. spelling, circus, recite	

Answer: 1. stood 2. cute 3. thought 4. gallop 5. (none)
6. (none) 7. tongue 8. through 9. eight 10. (none)
11. friendly 12. scout 13. thumb 14. bought 15. knob

5. The following words are written in the phonemic spelling discussed in this chapter. Read them and compare the phonemic spelling with the spelling in the conventional alphabet. (Only primary stresses are indicated.)

1. hóp	16. jə́jmənt	31. ból
2. bɔ́t	17. bə́tər	32. dɔ́n
3. θɔ́t	18. ʃúgər	33. fɔ́t
4. tɔ́t	19. ʃáɪn	34. lák
5. fǽtər	20. háʊs	35. lɔ́ki
6. bɛ́tər	21. múnlaɪt	36. fíl
7. mítər	22. flɔ́r	37. fílɪŋ
8. sít	23. blɔ́di	38. éti
9. sɪ́t	24. stúd	39. byúti
10. nídz	25. ʃúd	40. əbáʊt
11. əpráksɪmət	26. čə́rč	41. dəmákrəsi
12. réʃən	27. myútər	42. rítelz
13. wúnd(wáʊnd)	28. brɛ́dbaks	43. koápəret
14. ənɔ́f	29. gléʃər	44. yúənaɪ
15. húm	30. trɛ́ʒər	45. wɛndəðegohóm?

Answer: 1. hope 2. bought 3. thought 4. taught 5. fatter 6. better 7. meter 8. sit 9. seat 10. needs 11. approximate 12. ration 13. wound 14. enough 15. whom 16. judgment 17. butter 18. sugar 19. shine 20. house 21. moonlight 22. floor 23. bloody 24. stood 25. should 26. church 27. neuter 28. breadbox 29. glacier 30. treasure 31. bowl 32. dawn 33. fought 34. lock 35. lucky 36. fill 37. feeling 38. eighty 39. beauty 40. about 41. democracy 42. retails 43. cooperate 44. you and I 45. When do they go home?

5

The Forms
of Language:
English Morphology

We have already defined the *morpheme* as the smallest unit of speech to have some sort of recognizable meaning or function; it is the smallest possible meaningful building stone, made up of sound units, or *phonemes*. From the point of view of English at least, it seems useful to divide these morphemes into different categories: If we look at words like *prefix, precede, presume*, etc., we notice immediately that the unit *pre-* has been used over again in three words. There are many morphemes that function similarly to *pre-* as *prefixes*. Think of *con*tain, *con*duct, *con*strue; *ob*tain, *ob*ject; *re*tain, *re*ject; and so on. Other morphemes appear regularly at the end of the word as *suffixes*, usually characteristic of specific word classes. Thus the *suffix morpheme -al* reappears in adjectives: norm*al*, form*al*, glob*al*. Other examples of morphemes appearing as adjective endings are *-ous* (fam*ous*, odor*ous*, vapor*ous*); *-ic* (cub*ic*, metr*ic*, volcan*ic*); *-ful* (peace*ful*, faith*ful*, power*ful*); *-en* (wood*en*, gold*en*); etc. Other morphemes are characteristic of nouns: *-al* (this time reused as a noun morpheme: refus*al*, deni*al*, acquitt*al*); *-ure* (depart*ure*, fail*ure*); *-ment* (achieve*ment*, amuse*ment*, advertise*ment*); *-er* (help*er*, catch*er*, defend*er*); etc. Some suffixes that reoccur in verbs are *-ize* (liberal*ize*, equal*ize*); *-en* (dark*en*, cheap*en*, hard*en*); etc.

The most important morphemes are of course the *roots* themselves
to which the prefixes and suffixes are attached. Thus *-tain* is the
root being reused in *contain, detain, retain, sustain,* etc.; *-form* is the
root of *conform, reform, formal, formality.* The latter word actually
consists of three *morphemes:* the root *form,* the suffix *-al* (which forms
the adjective *formal*) and the suffix *-ity,* which is used to make the
noun *formality* from the adjective *formal.* There are quite a few roots
that follow the same pattern as *form* in being convertible to adjective
and noun according to the same model. Think of *norm* (*normal, nor-
mality*); *person* (*personal, personality*); etc.

In a class by themselves are also the morphemes that are the
grammatical endings and that are part and parcel of the grammatical
pattern of the sentence. We have already made the point that the
-s of the third person singular of verbs is a grammatical morpheme
characteristic of verbs: he think*s*, he like*s*, he make*s*. Just as characteristic of verbs are the endings *-ing* of he is smok*ing*, he is think*ing*,
etc. Also characteristic of verbs are the *-ed* of the past tense and of
the past participle: he smok*ed*, he laugh*ed*, he has smok*ed*, he has
laugh*ed*. Since these endings are restricted to a particular class of
words, we can of course use them to define the class. As far as
English is concerned, verbs are thus those words that take the endings *-s, -ing, -ed, -ed* (or their variants). The grammatical summary
that shows a word with all its possible grammatical endings is called
a *paradigm: laugh, laughs, laughing, laughed, laughed* is the paradigm of
laugh. Smoke, smokes, smoking, smoked, smoked is the paradigm of *smoke.*
And all the words that take the endings (or the variants of the
endings) illustrated in the above examples belong to the *paradigmatic
class of verbs.*

The *-s* which distinguishes the plural *cats* from the singular *cat* is
also a grammatical morpheme. (Note that it cannot be the same
grammatical morpheme as the *-s* of think*s*, since it does not mean
the same thing. It is the same *phoneme,* but the same sound or sounds
can have different meanings.) This *-s* is used regularly in English to
denote plurality of a certain class of words. These words all fall in
the pattern *cat/cats; hat/hats,* etc., and all the words that form a
plural by adding *-s* (or a variant of that morpheme) belong to the
paradigmatic class of nouns.

Still another paradigmatic class of English is represented by words
like *clever, happy,* etc. What is characteristic of the class is the pos-

sibility of adding the endings -*er* and -*est:* he is happi*er* than you, he is clever*er* than you; he is the happi*est;* he is the clever*est.* *Clever* and *happy* both belong to the *paradigmatic class of adjectives.*

The grammatical morphemes that we have discussed appear of course in the form of several variants (technical name: *allomorphs*). Some of these variants depend clearly on the sounds that precede the morphemes. For instance, if the noun ends in a voiced consonant like /b/, /d/, /g/, /v/, /m/, /n/, etc., the plural morpheme is /z/: *bug, bugs* (phonemically /bəgz/), *seed, seeds,* etc. The voiced /z/ is also used after vowels: *bee, bees* (/biz/); *sea, seas,* etc. If the noun ends in an unvoiced consonant, the unvoiced /s/ is used: *cat, cats* (/kæts/); *cup, cups.* After the consonant sounds /s/, /z/, /ʃ/, /ʒ/, /č/, /ǰ/, the plural morpheme becomes /əz/: *dish, dishes* (dɪʃəz): *witch, witches,* etc.

The endings of the verb paradigm have variants that are in a similar way predictable according to the "phonetic environment." Thus the /s/ of the third person singular verb follows the pattern of the /s/ noun plural. It is voiced after voiced consonant sounds: *reads* (/ridz/), *loves* (/ləvz/); it is unvoiced after unvoiced consonant sounds: *cuts* (/kəts/), *speaks* (/spiks/) and becomes /əz/ after the sibilant sounds: *wishes* (/wiʃəz/), catches (/kæčəz/). The -*ed* of the past and past participle is a voiced /d/ after voiced consonants: *rubbed* (/rəbd/), /t/ after unvoiced consonants: *laughed* (/læft/) and /əd/ after a /t/ or /d/: seated (/sitəd/).

Not all variants, or allomorphs, of the grammatical endings are neatly predictable according to the preceding sounds. English —like most other languages—has its share of irregular forms. Let us look, for instance, at singular/plural relationships like *ox/oxen, child/children, man/men, woman/women, foot/feet, goose/geese, mouse/mice, sheep/sheep,* etc. Such forms are a headache to the linguist who has to describe the plural morphemes involved (remember that they are *by definition* variants of the -*s* of *cat/cats*). They are of course even more of a headache to the person who has to learn English as a foreign language. The details of linguistic description need not concern us too much here, but let us point out that in a relation like *man/men* (mæn/mɛn) the /æ/ becomes then a singular indicator and the /ɛ/ a plural morpheme (variants of the -*s* in *cats*). This analysis of course raises the problem of what constitutes the root of the noun. Some have suggested that it is simply *m-n* and is therefore *discontinuous*—i.e., interrupted by the vowel that indicates the number. So far as the relationship between *sheep/sheep* is concerned, the plurality is obviously not indicated at all. In other words the alternate of *-s* in this particular case is nothing, or zero.

English plays similar tricks on the linguist and the language learner with the paradigm of the verb. If the paradigm of *laugh* is:

laugh   laughs   laughing   laughed   laughed

the paradigm of *give* is of course:

give   gives   giving   gave   given

Some other paradigms of English verbs are:

cut	cuts	cutting	cut	cut
creep	creeps	creeping	crept	crept
drive	drives	driving	drove	driven

and so on.

Since this book is written for the native speaker of English, we need not multiply the examples. It will be obvious that the variants in columns four and five (all allomorphs of the *-ed* of *laughed, laughed*) offers a serious problem of description (as well as of learning). Thus the *allomorph* of *-ed* involved in *gave* (/gev/) is the /e/ vowel sound (with *g-v* being the root?) and the allomorph represented by words like *cut* and *put* is again zero.

If we study the variants involved in the paradigm of the adjectives, we meet yet another type of problem. We have stated that the adjective paradigm follows the pattern *clever, cleverer, cleverest. He is clever; He is cleverer than you; He is the cleverest.* Clearly, in this pattern *clever, cleverer, cleverest* can be replaced by *good, better, best; bad, worse, worst.* Not only does the grammatical ending vary, but even the root morpheme is completely replaced by another root. Should we interpret *bett-* as a variant of *good?* We could—or we could simply say that *good* has been replaced by a different *root*, that *bett-* acts as a *replacive*. At any rate, the case of complete replacement of a morpheme is not uncommon in many languages and represents another problem to the linguist and obviously also to the learner of the language.

Once we realize that the root morpheme as well as the ending can be subject to considerable variation, or even complete replacement, we can isolate yet another paradigmatic class of English. If we look at sentences like *I see my brother; He is mine; He sees me,* we note that the words *I, me, my, mine* all have one meaning element (and therefore one morpheme) in common—namely, reference to the speaker or first person. They represent a paradigm—*I, me, my, mine* — in which the root meaning "first person" appears in different forms and with different endings. Just how to analyze these endings and how to describe them is rather difficult from the technical point of view. What is fairly obvious to the native speaker of English is that in the sample sentences chosen, *I, me, my, mine* could be replaced by the plural form *we, us, our, ours,* or by the second person forms *you, you, your, yours.* We can therefore note that the personal pronouns of English form a paradigm class represented by the arrangement:

I	me	my	mine
we	us	our	ours
you	you	your	yours
he	him	his	his

Note that just as in the table summarizing the verbal or adjectival paradigms, the root morpheme (although appearing in different variants) remains the same if we read the table horizontally. The grammatical morpheme, on the other hand, stays the same if we read the columns vertically. It may appear in different forms (variants, allomorphs) of course, but they are all different manifestations of the same morpheme.

Learning Exercises and Questions

1. How many morphemes are there in each of the following words?

1. comprehend	6. distribution	11. passable
2. legible	7. morpheme	12. illegible
3. indispensable	8. America	13. confer
4. oxen	9. vision	14. conference
5. construction	10. visual	15. difference

Answer: 1. two (com-prehend)   2. two (leg-ible)   3. four

(in-dis-pens-able) 4. two (ox-en) 5. three (con-struc-tion)
6. three (dis-tribu-tion) 7. two (morph-eme) 8. one
(America) 9. two (vis-ion) 10. two (vis-ual) 11. two (pass
-able) 12. three (il-leg-ible) 13. two (con-fer) 14. three
(con-fer-ence) 15. three (dif-fer-ence)

2. Give the paradigms of the following verbs:

   1. run   2. be   3. have   4. go

   Answer: 1. run, runs, running, ran, run   2. be, am, is, are,
   being, was, were, been   3. have, has, having, had, had   4. go,
   goes, going, went, gone

3. Give the paradigms of:

   1. she   2. they   3. it   4. who

   Answer: 1. she, her, her, hers   2. they, them, their, theirs
   3. it, it, its, its   4. who, whom, whose, whose

4. If we define adjectives and verbs as paradigmatic classes, what
   would be the reasons for considering:

   1. *beautiful* and *excellent* as belonging in a class different from
      that of adjectives like *happy* or *smart?*

   2. *ought* or *must* in a class different from that of regular verbs?

   Answer:

      1. *Beautiful* and *excellent* do not take the grammatical end-
         ings *-er*, *-est* (or any of their variants).

      2. *Ought* and *must* do not take any of the grammatical end-
         ings (or variants of endings) characteristic of other verbs:
         no third person singular ending, no *-ing* ending, no past
         tense, no part participle.

5. *-ness* is a morpheme that converts adjectives into nouns (e.g.,
   big/bigness). Give at least two more morphemes that serve the
   same function.

   Answer: *-ism* (ideal > idealism, real > realism); *-ity* (active >
   activity, false > falsity); *-th* (wide > width, warm > warmth)

6. A change in the voicing of the last consonant sound is a mor-

pheme converting nouns into verbs (e.g., *strife/strive*). Give at least four more examples of this morpheme.

Answer: bath>bathe; belief>believe; proof>prove; cloth>clothe; relief>relieve; grief>grieve

7. Give at least three examples (other than those mentioned in the text) of morphemes that are used to convert *nouns* into *adjectives*.

   Answer: *-en* (wood>wooden, gold>golden); *-ic* (history>historic, cube>cubic); *-ish* (book>bookish, fool>foolish); *-y* (bag>baggy, cloud>cloudy), etc.

8. In the sentence *The shapely girl looked at him happily*, the suffix (morpheme) *-ly* is used twice. Is it the same morpheme both times?

   Answer: No, because the two *-ly* forms do not have the same meaning or function. The *-ly* of *shapely* is a suffix that converts nouns into adjectives (shape>shapely, friend>friendly). The second *-ly* is used in the formation of adverbs: He is *happy*, he works *happily*. He is *steady*, he works *steadily*, etc.

9. What is the morpheme that is used to convert the noun *permit* to the verb *permit?* Give other examples of the same morpheme.

   Answer: The morpheme is the stress pattern. The noun has the stress pattern ÁCcent. The verb has the stress pattern acCENT. The individual stresses (′ ^ ` ˘) are phonemes, but their combinations, just like the combinations of other phonemes, are meaningful units and therefore morphemes. Other examples of the noun>verb shift brought about by the change in stress pattern are: súbjĕct>sŭbjéct, óbjĕct>ŏbjéct, áddrĕss>ăddréss.

6

Syntactical Patterns:

Some Examples

of English Syntax

A. PARTS OF SPEECH AND FUNCTION WORDS

The purpose of this discussion will be to introduce some of the concepts necessary for the understanding of syntactical patterning as exemplified by English. To give a complete discussion of English syntax would go far beyond the goals we have set ourselves. We have already pointed out that a pattern may be compared to some sort of blueprint. Building stones that can be exchanged for each other in the same place in the blueprint can be considered as belonging to the same class of word. In the preceding chapter we used the concept of a *paradigmatic class:* words that can take the same endings belong to the same class. Here we shall use the concept of *substitution class:* words that can be substituted for each other belong to the same class.

Let us look at the sentence: *The teacher prepared the lesson.* And now change the sentence by substituting different words:

The	*pupil*	prepared	the	lesson
The	*student*	prepared	the	lesson
The	student	*read*	the	lesson
The	student	*understood*	the	lesson
The	*boy*	understood	the	*book*
The	*child*	*bought*	the	book
The	*man*	bought	the	*house*

We can see that words like *student, boy, man*, etc., on the one hand, and *prepared, understood, bought*, etc., on the other are substitutable for each other: the first group belongs to the class of nouns, the second to the class of verbs. Thus if we wanted to use *N* as the abbreviation for *noun* and *V* as the abbreviation for *verb*, we could write some sort of formula like: *the* + *N* + *V* (past) + *the* + *N* and describe the pattern of the sentences that we have just created by the substitution process.

A sentence like: *The child feels sick* could, by a substitution process alone, be changed into sentences like:

The	child	looks	sick
The	boy	looks	intelligent
The	boy	seems	intelligent

Using *Adj.* for the substitution class of words by which we replaced *sick* in sentence 1, we could write the pattern of these sentences as *The* + *N* + *V* (present) + *Adj.*

Substituting in a sentence like: *The good child works well*, we might develop sentences like:

The	good	boy	works	quickly
The	intelligent	child	reads	fast
The	good	child	thinks	correctly
The	good	teacher	teaches	enthusiastically

The words that we could substitute for *well* in the initial sentence are of course all adverbs. Using *Adv.* as the abbreviation for adverb, we can thus describe the common pattern of all the above sentences as: *The* + *Adj.* + *N* (singular) + *V* (present) + *Adv.*

Nouns, adjectives, adverbs, and *verbs* are, in a sense, the main elements that make up the structure of English sentence patterns. But perhaps just as important are the endings and the function words that hold these main elements together. In the formulas we have developed thus far, we have kept the article *The* in the formula without replacing it by a general symbol. But we can of course replace *The* by other words just as we replaced the nouns, adjectives, adverbs, and verbs. Instead of saying *The boys worked hard*, we can say *All boys worked hard, Our boys worked hard*, etc. As a matter of fact there are quite a few words that could be put in place of *The* in a sentence like *The boy* (or *the boys*) *worked hard: any, some, more, many, eighteen, each,* etc. Now all of these words can be considered as belonging in the same *substitution class.* We shall call them *determiners* and use the abbreviation *det.* This makes the formula for the sentence *The boys worked hard: det.* $+ N$ (plural) $+ V$ (past) $+ Adv.$ The other function words of English can be quite similarly grouped into substitution classes. We shall do this only very briefly and for the most important classes.

A sentence like *The boys can work quickly* will help us to isolate function words called *auxiliaries* (*aux.*), namely, the words that can be substituted for *can: might, should, ought to, will, must,* etc. Our sample sentence thus follows the pattern: *det.* $+ N$ (plural) $+ aux.$ $+ V + Adv.$

In a sentence like *The boys worked rather quickly,* an entire group of words seems again substitutable for *rather: quite, awfully, too, more, most,* etc. We shall call them *intensifiers* (*int.*). *The boys worked rather quickly* is then an example of the pattern: *det.* $+ N$ (plural) $+ V$ (past) $+ int. + Adv.$

Another class of function words are the *linking words* (*link.*), words that combine or link words, phrases or sentences of equal status: *Your ideas seem interesting and helpful.* The sentence thus follows a pattern: *det.* $+ N$ (plural) $+ V$ (present) $+ Adj. + link. + Adj.$ Other function words belonging to this group are *neither, nor, or, not.*

The fifth group of function words that we shall point out comprises most of those words that you will probably recognize as *prepositions* (*prep.*). Take a sentence like *Charles must start at the top* [N (sing) $+ aux. + V + prep. + det. + N$ (sing)] and you will see that a variety of words like *on, with, across, by,* etc., are substitutable for *at.* All of these words—and others—make up the substitution class of *prepositions.*

Before leaving class 5, we should point out that connected with it is one of the trickiest problems of English grammar: namely, the so-called two-part verb and the connection between verb and preposition. Look at these sentences: *Charles gòt across the street* and *Charles got across his idea* or *Robert started up the street* and *Robert started up the car.* At first you might think that all of these sentences follow the same formula. But if you look more closely you will see that only the first sentence of each pair follows quite unambiguously the formula N (sing) $+ V$ (past) $+ prep. + det. + N$ (sing). The *across* of *Charles got across the street* seems replaceable by *to, into, through,* etc. The *up* of *started up the street* seems replaceable by *down, through,* etc. As far as the *got across* and *started up* of the second sentence of each pair is concerned, it seems preferable to consider them as one unit and to give them the formula: *N* (sing) + *V* (past) + *det.* + *N* (sing). As we have said, the problem is fairly complex. One way, however, by which you can usually tell whether you are dealing with a two-part verb or a verb followed by a preposition is the following: Replace the noun after the verb (or preposition) by a pronoun. In English grammar the pronouns are really capable of replacing nouns and belong to the same substitution class as the nouns. *Prepositions* thus stand before nouns and pronouns alike. In the sentence *He got across the street, the street* can be replaced by *it* and the *across* will remain before the *it: He got across it.* But if you want to use a pronoun instead of *the idea* of the *He got across his idea,* you will notice that it is clearly impossible to keep *across* before the replacement word. The sentence must become *He got it across.* This indicates that *across* as used in this sentence is not a *preposition* but that it should be considered as an integral part of the verb *to get across.*

The function words of the next class that we want to consider are words that might be substituted for *when* in a sentence like: *When can Charles come?* Words like *when, how, why* belong in this category. So do *who*(*m*) and *what*, although we have to change at least the verb of the original sentence to make them substitutable (*Whom* or *what can Charles see?*) We shall call this category *question words* (*qu.*).

The last group of function words we want to classify together are those that stand before groups which contain nouns and verbs; in other words, those function words that introduce subordinate clauses. These function words (*subordinators, sub.*) are quite numerous: *after, because, whenever,* etc. The formula of a sentence like *Robert left only after his friend arrived* is thus *N* (sing) + *V* (past) + *Adv.* + *sub.* + *det.* + *N* (sing) + *V* (past). In connection with these subordinators, let us point out that it is of course possible for the same word to belong to different substitution classes. Quite a few of the subordinators are also prepositions. *He left after my friend and after Charles arrived* shows *after* first as a *preposition* and then as a *subordinator.*

There are yet various other groups of function words which we shall not discuss in detail. Just to give a few examples: Words like *yes, no, o.k.,* seem to form a group by themselves. So do the "attention getters" like *look, say, listen.* Of course let us remember again that words may belong to more than one category. Thus *look, say,* etc. belong in the substitution (and paradigmatic) class of verbs, but when used as a single utterance they seem to function differently from the way in which they perform in the sentence structure. Other examples of a double function are the words *not* and *there.* We have mentioned already the word *not* as a linking word (*He plays well, not brilliantly*). If *not* is used as the negative of the verb, however, it operates in a slightly different way and in a function in which it does not seem replaceable by any other word. If in the sentence *He does not play well* we replaced *not* by an adverb like *always*, the *does* (used only with the expression of negation) would also change its function, become stressed, and convey a meaning of emphasis that it does not, indeed, convey in the original sentence.

The word *there* is usually an adverb. In a sentence like: *Why do you work there?* it could be replaced by *here, now, badly,* etc. But in the expressions *there is, there are . . . ,* it seems to fulfill its own unique function: e.g., *How many students are there in the class? There are twenty-seven of them.* The *there* used in the preceding sentences is not replaceable by any other adverbs. There are, so to speak, two words *there* in the English language: the adverb (*He is here, not there*) and the function word of the *there is, there are* formula.

The so-called auxiliary verbs *have, do, be* are also, in a sense, in a class by themselves. At any rate they illustrate very well the principle of possible multiple function. The verb *be* can in some ways function like any other verb that is capable of being followed by an adjective. The *is* of *He is intelligent* can be changed to *seems, looks, appears,* etc. However in the so-called "progressive tense" construction (*He is working; We were wondering*) the verb *to be* functions uniquely and in a separate class. This double aspect of function applies quite similarly to *do* and *have.* *Do* functions sometimes like an ordinary verb: *He does his homework. Does* can be replaced by *prepares, knows, understands,* etc., but there are, so to speak, at least two more words *to do* in the English language. One is the *do* used for emphasis: *They do do their homework.* The other is the *do* of the question and negation construction: *Do they do their homework? No, they do not do their homework.* The verb *have*, finally, can also operate as a normal verb: e.g., *I have a car. Have* may be replaced by *own, buy, sell,* etc. Quite distinct from this verb, *have* is the function word that has at least three distinct functions. (1) It expresses the *completion* of an action: *I have bought a car.* (2) It expresses *necessity: I have to buy a car; I have to have a car.* (3) It is used to convey the idea of *causation: I have my brother do the work, I shall have this done by him,* etc.

Learning Exercises

1. Write out the formulas according to which the following sentences are constructed (use the abbreviations suggested in the text: *det., aux., int., link., prep., qu., sub., N, V, Adj., Adv.*):

   1. The boy did not understand the answer.
   2. Our new teacher arrived yesterday.
   3. This boy can understand you quite well.
   4. Every man must speak out for himself.
   5. We have many interesting friends.
   6. Why did Charles run down the street?
   7. You should give up the whole idea.
   8. Charles did not do his assignment.
   9. There is no hope for you.

   Answer: 1. det. + N + did + not + V + det. + N   2. det. + Adj. + N + V + Adv.   3. det. + N + aux. + V + N + int. + Adv.   4. det. + N + aux. + V + prep. + N   5. N + V + det. + Adj. + N (plural)   6. qu. + did + N + V + prep. + det. + N   7. N + aux. + V + det. + Adj. + N   8. N + did + not + V + det. + N   9. there + is + det. + N + prep. + N

2. For each of the sentences in the preceding exercise, write out one sentence that uses the same pattern but different words. (Words not abbreviated in the formulas, e.g., *did, not,* etc., should stay the same.)

   Sample Answers: 1. Our child did not read this book. 2. This old man came late. 3. My son will follow Robert immediately. 4. Any soldier will fight for freedom. 5. Robert knows several beautiful girls. 6. Why did you return with your uncle? 7. We must study our new lesson. 8. We did not follow your advice. 9. There is a rumor about Charles.

B. TRANSFORMATIONS

One way of describing the sentence structures of English would be to determine all the possible types of sentences and write down all their formulas. The complete inventory of all the formulas would then be a complete description of English structures. Yet there is still another way of approaching the task. The other approach proceeds from the assumption that there are a limited number of patterns that are basic and that all other patterns can be derived from them by successive changes or transformations. The basic patterns, so to speak, imply the others.

Thus one might say that pattern $N + V + N$ (John loves Mary) implies or can be transformed into $N + is + V$ (*past part.*) $+ by + N$ (Mary is loved by John). It is important to realize that in this kind of description the basic pattern implies the one into which it can be transformed. The direction of the transformation, however, cannot necessarily be reversed. The construction *det.* $+ N + V + Adj.$ (the boy looks intelligent) implies or can be transformed into *det.* $+ Adj.$ $+ N$ (the intelligent boy). But not every construction *det.* $+ Adj.$ $+ N$ can necessarily be transformed into a construction of the type *det.* $+ N + V + Adj.$ *The principal cause, the chief reason, the main idea* cannot be utilized in sentences like *The cause is principal, The reason is chief*, etc.

The above examples show yet another advantage of the transformation approach. Evidently the transformations make explicit certain peculiarities of language that are not revealed by the formulas' descriptions. *The principal reason* or *the intelligent reason* both follow the formula *det.* $+ Adj.$ $+ N$. But the fact that *the principal reason* cannot be transformed into a sentence like *the reason is principal* makes it clear that *principal* and *intelligent* do not belong to the same class after all—or that at least the class "Adjective" is in need of further subdivision.

Sentences of the type *John became my friend* or *John killed the horse* will further illustrate the point. Both sentences follow the pattern $N + V$ (*past*) $+ det.$ $+ N$. *John killed the horse* can be transformed into the passive: *The horse was killed by John.* The sentence *John became my friend* is not capable of a passive transformation. Of course at this point you will say that you knew this all along; or you might add that *killed* is a transitive verb, while *became* is not. This is of course just another way of saying that as a native speaker of English you know which words can be put into the passive and which cannot. A foreigner learning English would have to be told, and words like *become* would have to be pointed out to him as belonging to a category different from *kill;* and—to stress again—the important fact that these words are a special category is made explicit only by the application of the transformation.

To give one more example of the insufficiency of the formula, take the three sentences: *The man gave the child a necklace; The director considered his subordinate an idiot; The people elected his brother our leader.* The formula behind those three sentences is again the same: *det.* + *N* + *V (past)* + *det.* + *N* + *det.* + *N.* In the first sentence both of the noun objects can become the subject of a passive transformation (change the verb into the corresponding form of *be* plus the past participle of the verb): *The child was given a necklace by the man. A necklace was given to the child by the man.* In the second and third sentences, only the first noun following the verb can become the subject of a passive transformation; *His subordinate was considered, His brother was elected,* etc. Only in the second sentence does it seem possible to replace the final noun by an adjective: *The director considered his subordinate stupid.* Thus the transformation has shown again that the formula hides many distinctions and that for the purpose of a complete description we must introduce subcategories into classifications like *Noun, Verb, Adjective,* etc.

The criteria applied in forming paradigmatic or substitution classes have already allowed us to consider words like *have, may, can, might* in separate categories: *may, can, ought, should* do not take the third person singular-*s* of regular verbs. Only *have* can be used before the past participle of the verb to express completed action. The consideration of the negative and interrogative transformation formulas furnishes yet another reason for grouping these words in a separate category. Observe the following transformations. *Charles works; Charles does not work; Does Charles work?* as opposed to: *Charles may work; Charles may not work; May Charles work?*

The normal verbs of English use the auxiliary *do* to create their negative and interrogative patterns. The auxiliary verbs (*have, be, might, should, may, can, will,* etc.) do not use *do,* but form the negative with the simple addition of *not* plus the interrogative by a simple reversal of word order, putting the subject after the verb.

Yet another way to think of transformation is to consider it as a possibility of expanding basic sentences. This expansion procedure can be applied to any part of a basic sentence. Let us consider a few examples of expanding the verb or noun element of basic sentences. Some of the simplest ways of expanding the verb are the following:

1. A simple form of a verb [e.g., *think(s)*, *drink(s)*, *play(s)*] can be expanded by preceding it with an auxiliary: *Robert works hard* or *We work hard* can be changed into *Robert may (should, could, might, will, ought to,* etc.*) work hard. We (shall, would, might,* etc.*) work hard.*

2. A simple word form can be replaced by *have (has)* plus the past participle: *I work, I have worked; We should work, We should have worked; He must work, He must have worked.*

3. The simple tenses of most verbs (*works, work, worked*) can be changed into the progressive tense (*be* + the *-ing* form of the verb): *I write, I am writing; Charles played, Charles was playing,* etc. Here we note again, however, that the transformation spells out a certain group of verbs with which the progressive tense transformation is, typically at least, impossible. Could you apply it to: *We know the answer; We understand the truth; We are in Paris; We have money; We believe your answer,* etc.? In other words, English has a limited number of verbs—typically expressing a state rather than an action—which do not appear in the progressive forms.

Perhaps the most obvious way of expanding the verb section of the sentence consists of adding an adverb—or a subordinate clause (which, so to speak, may replace an adverb). Thus *Charles arrived* can be expanded to: *Charles arrived yesterday* or *Charles arrived yesterday after dinner;* and *after dinner* can be thought of as being replaced by *after we had dinner.* So the expanded sentence finally reads: *Charles arrived yesterday after we had dinner.* (Note that the subordinate clause *after we had dinner* can be explained as having been derived from the main clause *we had dinner.* Most main clauses can be transformed into a subordinate clause by having it begin with a conjunction, one of the *subordinators.*)

Expansion of the noun part of the sentence to "noun clusters" can

take place in a similar way. We can add an adjective or a prepositional phrase: *The boy is here; The good boy is here; The good boy from
New York is here.* In English any element that fits into the empty slot
of the pattern *N + is (are)* . . . can be used to create a noun cluster
by simply adding it to the noun. Thus we can say that the expression
The boy is over there or *The boy is to my right* implies the noun clusters:
The boy over there or *The boy to my right* and can be used to transform
the sentence: *The boy is intelligent* to *The boy over there is intelligent* or
The boy to my right is intelligent. Of course noun clusters can also be
created by adding subordinate clauses to the noun. Noun clauses
can be constructed out of main clauses by replacing the noun subjects by *who(m), that, which,* and the noun object by *who, that, which,*
or by dropping it altogether. *The man came* then becomes *who came;
I saw the man* becomes *whom I saw,* or . . . *I saw,* etc.

These subordinate clauses are then utilized to expand nouns to
clusters: *The man is lying* becomes *The man (whom) I saw is lying* or
The man who came was lying, etc. Yet another way of creating a subordinate sentence for the construction of noun clauses consists of replacing the *determiners,* which precede the noun by the expression
whose: The child had died can thus be changed to *whose child had died*
and be used to expand a sentence like: *The mother cried* to *The mother,
whose child had died, cried.*

Of course, one cannot really claim that a speaker of English who
says *The mother, whose child had died, cried* has consciously taken the
two sentences *The mother cried* and *The child died* and combined and
transformed them into one. The description of the language as a
process of transforming from the simple to the complex is probably
a device of the grammarian; but this does not take away from its use-
fulness, especially if the language you are dealing with is not your
native language. Description in terms of "transforming" or "gen-
erating" new sentences out of familiar ones simply drives home the
fact that grammar is not simply a set of dead rules, but is above all
the tool that you must use in *creating* sentences.

Learning Exercises

1. Expand the verb of each of the following sentences by (1) preceding it with an *auxiliary*, then (2) replacing the simple verb
   by *have* plus the *past participle.*

1. Charles knows the answer.   3. We follow your advice.
2. Robert understands me.   4. Our friends help us.

Sample Answers: 1. Charles may know the answer. Charles may have known the answer. 2. Robert should understand me. Robert should have understood me. 3. We ought to follow your advice. We ought to have followed your advice. 4. Our friends should help us. Our friends should have helped us.

2. Expand the noun subject of the following sentences by adding an adjective and a subordinate clause:

1. This man knows the answer.
2. Our friend will help us.
3. The solution is difficult.
4. This language is difficult.

Sample Answers: 1. This noble man whom we trust knows the answer. 2. Our good friend who has helped us before will help us. 3. The final solution that you expect is difficult. 4. This beautiful language which you have studied is difficult.

3. Transform the following sentences into the passive:

1. Robert gave Charles the money.
2. The class elected Charles president.
3. John understood my orders.
4. We consider Charles our leader.

Answer: 1. Charles was given the money by Robert. The money was given to Charles by Robert. 2. Charles was elected president by the class. 3. My orders were understood by John. 4. Charles is considered our leader by us.

4. In the text we stated that *seem, give, elect, consider* really belong to different classes of verbs. Give at least two more examples for each of these classes.

Answer: 1. Seem: become, look, feel, grow   2. Give: send, write   3. Elect: vote, choose   4. Consider: think, believe

5. The construction *The boy seems intelligent* implies the construction *the intelligent boy;* the construction *I know the boy* implies in

a similar way *whom I know.* Both of these can be used to expand
the noun to a noun nucleus in the sentence *The boy will help you*
to *The intelligent boy whom I know will help you.* In a similar way
combine the following sentences:

1. The child looks sad. You are looking at the child. The child
is my brother.   2. The man looks old. His beard blew in the
wind. The man looked at us.

Answer: 1. The sad child you are looking at is my brother.
2. The old man whose beard blew in the wind looked at us.

6. Study the way in which the following three constructions can
be transformed and combined into one:

1. The boy is over there > The boy over there
2. His mother studies French > whose mother studies French
3. The other children like the boy > The boy is liked by the
other children

*The boy over there whose mother studies French is liked by the other
children.*

On the model of the above example, transform the following
sentences and combine them into one construction:

(a) 1. The man is to my left.
     2. His hand is bleeding.
     3. Everybody stares at the man.

(b) 1. The soldiers are from New York.
     2. Their noise became louder and louder.
     3. The guests asked the soldiers to leave.

Answer:

(a) 1. The man to my left   2. whose hand is bleeding
     3. The man is stared at by everybody

     *The man to my left whose hand is bleeding is stared at by
     everybody.*

(b) 1. The soldiers from New York   2. whose noise be-
     came louder and louder   3. The soldiers were asked
     by the guests to leave

     *The soldiers from New York whose noise became louder and
     louder were asked by the guests to leave.*

7. Observe how the following sentences are transformed and combined into one construction:

1. Policemen swing clubs > Club-swinging policemen
2. Policemen tried to disperse the crowd > who tried to disperse the crowd
3. The people attacked the policemen > the policemen were attacked by the people
4. They reached the platform > when they reached the platform

   Club-swinging policemen who tried to disperse the crowd were attacked by the people when they reached the platform.

On the model of the above example, transform the following sentences and combine them into one construction:

1. Party members carry cards.
2. Party members had received orders to organize a strike.
3. The police arrested the party members.
4. They arrived at the meeting.

Answer: 1. Card-carrying party members 2. who had received orders to organize a strike 3. The party members were arrested by the police 4. when they arrived at the meeting

Card-carrying party members who had received orders to organize a strike were arrested by the police when they arrived at the meeting.

III

The Problems of
Foreign Language
Learning

7

Pronunciation

Problems

Let us first take a more detailed look at the pronunciation problems involved in foreign language learning. Here we can first of all distinguish those problems that we might call genuine pronunciation problems from those that can be classified as spelling pronunciation problems. A genuine pronunciation problem exists if the learner has difficulty making the required sound. A spelling pronunciation problem occurs if the sound is not really difficult as such, but the learner is misled by the spelling. We could define a spelling pronunciation mistake as a mistake you would not make at all if you did not know how to write the foreign language. The cause for the error may lie in the native or in the foreign language. Thus a foreigner learning English may associate the symbol *ch* with the sound /ʃ/ (as in *she* /ʃi/), customarily spelled *ch* in his language (for example, the French word **chaise** is pronounced /ʃɛz/). Although perfectly capable of pronouncing the sound /č/ (as in *chin* /čɪn/), he may thus say /ʃɪn/ (for *chin*) or /ʃərʃ/ (instead of /ʃčərč/) for *church*. The cause for the spelling pronunciation may naturally be also an inconsistency of sound-symbol correspondence in the language to be learned. Thus the relative inconsistency of English spelling is likely to cause numerous spelling pronunciation problems for foreigners learning English (it does even with native speakers!). But a foreigner who has learned to pronounce *head* as /hɛd/ may very well apply his hard-earned knowledge in pronouncing *heal* as /hɛl/—and the use of the same spelling for words like *lead* (simple form of verb /lid/) and *lead* (noun or past form of verb /lɛd/) seems nothing short of a special form of torture devised to mislead the native and confound the foreigner.

Even so, spelling pronunciation problems are generally more easily conquered than genuine pronunciation problems created by the inability to pronounce the particular sound. Here again we note that all of language depends on a system. A sound that a person is capable of pronouncing easily within his native system may become difficult merely because it is used differently within the foreign language system (although it is indeed the same sound that exists in his native language). We have already mentioned the fact that the sound /ŋ/ (siNG) may be a very difficult sound for you at the beginning of a word. You would have great difficulty pronouncing the sound if you had to learn a language which has words like *ŋa*, *ŋo*, etc., although the phoneme /ŋ/ does exist in English. A similar situation of a familiar sound suddenly becoming difficult may arise if the sound exists as a variant in the system of the learner, but becomes an independent phoneme in the language to be learned. As a native speaker of English you say an unaspirated /p/, /t/, /k/ (without puff of air—see page 22) after /s/. Can you say the same kind of /p/, /t/, /k/ in any other position? Probably not. It would take quite a bit of practice for you to be able to transpose the /p/ of *spin* to the pronunciation of *pin*, *pie*, etc. The fact that the /p/ of *spin* is unaspirated will not automatically assure that you can say the same kind of /p/ correctly in languages in which it is required in all positions. And if you were to learn a language in which the /p/ of *spin* and that of *pin* were different and distinct phonemes, you would again be in trouble. Most likely you would not only have a problem in pronouncing the sounds correctly, but you would also have difficulty in hearing the difference between the two sounds.

In the majority of pronunciation problems of course the difficulty is created simply by the absence of the sound in the native language. What is most likely to happen in that case is that the learner substitutes a sound—usually the "nearest" sound of the native language. The foreigner whose native language does not know the /θ/ sound of *thin* will substitute /s/ or /t/: *thin* becomes *tin* or *sin*. Such sound substitutions are of course always undesirable. Just how "bad" or serious they are depends on the amount of confusion they create. Since /s/ and /t/ are phonemes of English, the substitution of either one for /θ/ may create a lot of confusion and impair the clarity of communication. Any sound substitution which obliterates the distinctions between phonemes of the language is serious. A sound substitution that merely changes the pronunciation of a sound without making it "collide" with another phoneme of the system is more acceptable, although it is still a sign of a foreign accent. If, for instance, a speaker of a foreign language pronounces English /t/ always as a dental (remember that English /t/ is alveolar) and without aspiration, his way of saying *time, two, tea*, etc., may sound strange, but would be perfectly clear and comprehensible.

In order to make the problem of native language interference more real, let us go together through three short experiments in "interfering" with the pronunciation of English.

1. (a) Assume that the learner of English has no /θ/ and /ð/ sounds ("th" sounds) in his language, and substitutes /s/ (*see*) and /z/ (*zinc*). Pronounce *the, that, those, teeth*, and *thin* with his accent.

(b) Assume that in his language all final consonant sounds are *unvoiced:* /d/ is pronounced /t/, /b/ is pronounced /p/, /v/ is pronounced /f/, etc. Pronounce in this way *good, was, tub, gave*, and *bad*.

(c) The language of the learner has no /w/ sound. The sound /v/ (*van*) is the nearest substitute: Say *winter, water, when*, and *wait*.

Now see whether you can combine all of these three speech peculiarities or interference phenomena and pronounce the following sentences with the accent of your "problem student":

We give the child the money. He did not understand what we were thinking at the moment. Could you please help them? This is a very good idea.

You have by now perhaps realized that these mispronunciations are typical of a German accent in English. Now let us try to imitate a different accent.

2. (a) The language of the learner has no sound /ɪ/ (as in *bit*) and no sound /ʊ/ (as in *good*). Instead he uses sounds like the /i/ sound (of

b*ea*t) and the /u/ sound (of f*oo*d). Pronounce the words s*i*t, f*i*t, d*i*d, g*oo*d, sh*ou*ld, st*oo*d using these substitutions.

(b) There is no phonemic difference between /v/ and /b/ in his language. The sound for both of them is like English /b/ in initial position and somewhat like English /v/ between vowels. Now pronounce *v*alid, *v*ain, *v*acuum, *v*acancy, ru*bb*er, ro*b*ot.

(c) The combination of *s* plus consonant cannot be pronounced without a preceding vowel. Pronounce the /ɛ/ sound before *S*panish, *s*tand, *s*tone, *s*chool.

(d) There is no phonemic difference between an unvoiced /s/ sound (hi*ss*) and the voiced sound /z/ (hi*s*). The voiced sound /z/ occurs only before other voiced consonants. This means that in all other positions the unvoiced /s/ is used. Pronounce the following with unvoiced /s/: Mi*ss*ouri, Loui*s*iana, ama*z*ing.

Now combine again the four interference phenomena and apply them simultaneously to the following sentences:

I thi*n*k that *S*pani*s*h i*s* ea*s*y. Engli*s*h i*s* *v*ery d*i*ff*i*cult. I like *s*trawberrie*s* *v*ery much. The *v*isiti*n*g *s*tudents are *v*ery lazy.

The above mispronunciations do not illustrate all of the possible difficulties of the native speaker of (yes, you guessed it!) Spanish in English, but they do show some of his main troubles.

3. For the final experiment let us assume that

(a) The learner cannot distinguish between /ɪ/ and /i/, /ʊ/ and /u/ (as in experiment 2 above), and substitutes /i/ (b*ea*t) for /ɪ/ (b*i*t) and /u/ (f*oo*d) for /ʊ/ (g*oo*d).

(b) Now try the following trick: In English one syllable of each word has a heavy (primary) accent: *difficult* is pronounced díffĭcŭlt (see page 38). See whether you can say words like *difficult, pronunciation, fluently, English* without primary stress, but allotting the same amount of stress and time to every syllable: díffícúlt, flúéntlý pronounced with the same timing and stress that you would use in counting óne, twó, thrée.

Now, substituting /i/ and /u/ for /ɪ/ and /ʊ/, say:

Í i*s* díffícúlt tó speák Énglí*s*h. Cóme wíth me a*n*d stúdý Frénch. Ít í*s* á beáutífúl lánguáge.

Learning Exercises

1. 1. In language *X* the sounds /l/ and /r/ are variants of the same phoneme: /l/ is pronounced initially, /r/ in all other positions. How might a speaker of language *X* pronounce the following: "Hello, Robert. Please lend me your flashlight."?

    2. In language *Y*, the sounds /p/ and /f/ are variants of the same phoneme: /p/ is pronounced initially, /f/ in all other positions. How might a speaker of language *Y* pronounce the following: It was difficult to find a furnished room near the campus for the person who was offered the fellowship.?

    Answer: 1. Hero, Lobert. Prease lend me your frashright. 2. It was difficult to pind a purnished room on the camfus por the person who was offered the pellowshif.

2. A "minimal pair" is made up of two words that are distinguished by only *one* phoneme (*mat/map*, *bit/pit*, *map/mop*, etc.). Think of some minimal pairs in English that would merge completely in the speech of a foreigner who could not make the difference between:

    1. /i/ and /ɪ/   3. /s/ and /θ/
    2. /æ/ and /ɛ/   4. /s/ and /z/

    Sample Answer: 1. seat/sit; beat/bit; feat/fit; lead/lid; sheep/ship 2. bat/bet; man/men; Dan/den; sad/said; lag/leg 3. sigh/thigh; sing/thing; sank/thank; saw/thaw; sick/thick 4. seal/zeal; lacy/lazy; rice/rise; sue/zoo; loose/lose

3. Give some pairs of words that might be confused with each other in the speech of a learner who

    1. cannot distinguish between /e/ and /ɛ/.
    2. cannot distinguish voiced and unvoiced consonants at the end of the word.
    3. cannot distinguish voiced and unvoiced stops in word initial position.

Sample Answer: 1. bait/bet; late/let; sale/sell; pain/pen;
laid/led 2. rib/rip; rid/writ; pig/pick; dug/duck; leaf/
leave; seed/seat; belief/believe; ridge/rich 3. pin/bin; time/
dime; could/good; dial/tile; pet/bet; probably also Jane/
chain; gin/chin

8

The Problems

of Morphology

In the area of morphology the interference factor is probably less important than in the other levels of structure. Typically, the reason for using a wrong form (wrong in the sense that it is put together incorrectly) lies in confusion created by the language to be learned rather than in some sort of mix-up caused by the native language of the learner. Languages follow certain patterns—in word formation as well as in grammatical paradigms—and the foreigner learning the language may often make the wrong choice of pattern, very much like the small child who says "gived," "speaked," etc.

Let us first take another look at a few examples of patterning in word formation and the possible results of misapplied extensions of patterns.

Example 1

norm	normal	normality
form	formal	formality
brute	brutal	brutality
cause	causal	causality
coast	coastal	—
option	optional	—

Note that the extension of the complete pattern to "coast" would give a word "coastality," which impresses any speaker of English as complete nonsense; "optionality" isn't quite that bad (though it is not found in the dictionary). Of course historically many words have been created by extending patterns like the above to words to which they did not previously apply; yet the process of extension by analogy (a very frequent process in word formation and grammar, from the historical point of view) is not acceptable if applied by the nonnative learner.

Example 2

freak	freakish
book	bookish
sheep	sheepish

duck   —

Example 3

fame	famous
pomp	pompous
vapor	vaporous

steam   —

Example 4

dust	dusty
fun	funny
rain	rainy
noise	noisy
water	watery

quiet   —

Example 5

friend	friendly
man	manly
sister	sisterly
mother	motherly
cost	costly

aunt   —

Example 6

angel	angelic
cube	cubic
rhythm	rhythmic

space   —

Of course the derivational endings used in the above examples have specific meanings: *-ous* means something like "full of," *-ly* means "in the manner of," etc. To realize these meanings is of course quite important; but even the knowledge of the meaning does not change the fact that the possibility or impossibility of using the endings seems, for English at least, somewhat unpredictable. If we can say *sheep/sheepish*, why not *duck/duckish, cow/cowish?* Just as unpredictable is often the possibility of switching from one word class into the other by simply using the word in a different function or applying the morphological, grammatical endings of the other class. Thus English offers in many cases the possibility of making a verb out of a noun by simply using it as such; in other words the same word can be either a noun or a verb: I am opening a *can* of tomatoes; I am going to *can* some tomatoes. Yet this rule, which often works, does not work all the time. You can eat *breakfast* and *lunch*, and you can *lunch* and *breakfast;* you can eat *dinner* and *supper*, but you cannot *dinner* and *supper* (however, you can *dine* and *sup*).

The havoc created by the wrong extension of grammatical pattern is even more obvious. Here again we should stress that the learner is often only continuing a process which has been going on for centuries, namely the extension of the more frequent, dominant, or "productive" grammatical patterns into areas where they have not yet been applied. Centuries ago English had many more plurals of the type *oxen* (ox), *geese* (goose), or past tenses like *brought* (bring), *sang* (sing). These types have gradually been losing ground in favor of the plurals in -*s* and the past tenses in -*ed*. This, however, does not make plurals like *childs, oxes, gooses*, etc., or past tenses like *bringed, thinked, singed*, etc., sound any better if they are created by a nonnative speaker.

Similar to the wrong extension of a paradigm is the use of a root in a form in which the language has replaced it by another root morpheme: *Good, better, best; go, went, gone*, etc. are not the patterns that one would expect. Yet another possibility of error lies in extending the correct ending to a word class that does not, in fact, use the ending at all; we have already pointed out that technically words like *excellent* and *beautiful* do not belong in the paradigmatic class of adjectives: Mary may be *prettier* than Jane, but at least as far as English is concerned, she cannot be *beautifuller*.

When it comes to the wrong extension of grammatical endings to words where they do not belong, the interference factor—in other words the native language of the learner—may come into play. To give some obvious examples that one can hear quite frequently from nonnative learners of English: many languages use verb endings in all tenses—English has for all practical purposes only one verb ending, the -*s* morpheme (or its variants) for the third person singular present. Many nonnatives will extend this -*s* as a third person marker into the past tense: *He wrotes to me.* In many languages the equivalents of English *can, must*, etc., are "real" verbs insofar as they take the conjugational endings. Thus *He can understand me* may become *He cans understand me.* English marks its plural only in the noun, never in the adjective. Many languages have plural forms in the adjective and insist on agreement between the noun and the adjective that modifies it, as for instance: *The intelligents boys are always readies.*

Learning Exercises

1. Make up some "impossible" words that a nonnative speaker of English might create by misapplying the suffix-morphemes:

   1. -ic   2. -ous   3. -ly

   Sample Answer: 1. famic, vaporic   2. reputationous, cubous   3. firely, sheeply

2. Explain briefly the reason for the errors found in the following sentences (real examples taken from nonnative learners of English):

   1. He will can do this.
   2. They look at yous with great amusity.
   3. Charles brang home some beautifuls dishs.
   4. He spokes not very goodly.

   Answer: 1. *can* treated like a verb instead of a function word (auxiliary verb).   2. *yous*—plural morpheme attached to the pronoun (notice the same tendency in slang: *youse guys!*); derivational suffix -*ity* (*animosity*, etc.) misapplied.   3. *brang*—past tense formed on the model of *sing; beautifuls*—adjective put into plural; *dishs*—wrong variant of the plural morpheme, /s/ instead of /əz/.   4. -*s* ending transposed to past tense; root morpheme *good* kept instead of replacive *well*.

9

Vocabulary

Problems

Morphological problems result in the learner making up a wrong word. On the other hand, very often the learner simply uses a word in the wrong way; in other words, the word itself is correct, but the learner misunderstands its function or meaning. The reason for this kind of mistake is invariably that the learner has simply equated a foreign word with a word of his native language, and used it in exactly the same way. However, words in one language really never mean another word in another language, not if by "mean" we understand that they will correspond to each other in any or all circumstances. As a matter of fact, one could say that a word used by itself in isolation does not really mean anything, for it is used without context and without referring to something that a speaker wants to express. Even words like *cat* or *dog* do not mean anything unless they are applied in a specific situation. If I make the statement *I am taking my dog for a walk*, I am referring to an animal, and *dog* "means" this particular animal. If, in a rage, I call somebody a "dirty dog," *dog* "means" something quite different. A word—unless it is applied in a specific situation—has no meaning, but only a *range* or *potential of meanings;* and the range or potential of any word in any language is hardly ever identical with the potential meanings of a word in another language.

We have already pointed out the type of error that arises if the meaning of one word is equated with the meaning of another. For the sake of a few more illustrations, let us imagine that English is divided into two languages: English A and English B. On the basis of "translating" a sentence from English A into English B, we shall establish word correspondences between English A and English B and see what happens if we translate on the basis of the correspondence.

Example 1

English A: Charles and Jane quarreled. Then they *made up.*
English B: Charles and Jane quarreled. Then they *became conciliated.*

Conclusion: *made up = became conciliated*

English A: Charles and John made up the exam.
English B: ?

Example 2

English A: The rebel leader had to *get out of* the country.
English B: The rebel leader had to *leave* the country.

Conclusion: *get out of = leave*

English A: What did you *get out of* this book?
English B: ?

Example 3

English A: The army *took up* its position.
English B: The army *occupied* its position.

Conclusion: *took up = occupied*

English A: Charles took up mathematics.
English B: ?

Such examples could easily be multiplied. The main point to remember is simply that just because one statement is the translation of another statement, the two statements do not necessarily contain words that are the equivalent of each other. We could say, for instance, that a sentence like *I don't quite understand this* (English A) could be translated *This isn't really very clear to me* (English B). Which word in the sentence of English B "means" *understand?* Which word "means" *don't?* Sentences of different languages very often correspond to each other in just the same way as the two English sentences that we have just given as examples. To draw the conclusion from such correspondences in the total meaning of sentences that there are also words within the sentences that must be each other's exact counterparts is quite unwarranted and will usually lead to rather obvious errors.

The errors caused by establishing word-to-word correspondences are especially serious if the words involved are function words signalling grammatical relationships. Again let us give a few examples using English A and English B.

Example 1

English A: The book *which* I gave him. . . .
English B: The book *that* I gave him. . . .

             Conclusion: *which* = *that*

English A: I don't know *that.*
English B: ?

Example 2

English A: I can do this *too.*
English B: I can do this *also.*

             Conclusion: *too* = *also*

English A: This is much *too* difficult.
English B:

Example 3

English A: I *have to* write this book.
English B: I *must* write this book.

             Conclusion: *have to* = *must*

English A: Charles will *have to* leave.
English B: ?

A somewhat special type of vocabulary problem arises in the case of so-called *idioms.* Idioms may be defined as expressions that do not have the meaning one might expect them to have according to their component parts: expressions like *I have a frog in my throat, I got a kick out of his answer, He sure put his foot in his mouth that time,* etc. are likely to convey meanings that are not at all clear if we interpret the statements literally as being made up of the meaning of their components. Obviously idioms of this type cannot be duplicated literally in another language. As a matter of fact, the literal translation of an idiom of the native language into the foreign is not a very frequent cause of error in foreign language learning. The native speaker is usually aware of the fact that he is manipulating his own language in a special way and does not attempt to give to his idiom a literal foreign language translation. Such literal translations are usually attempted as jokes, but only seldom are they the cause of unintentional error (you don't *really* think that *I get a kick out of this book* could be translated literally into French or Spanish—and mean any thing sensible). The real problem created by idioms lies in the idiomatic expressions of the foreign language to be learned, because the latter are bound to create serious problems of comprehension and misunderstanding. The author of this book remembers quite vividly the shocked expression on the face of the Spaniard who had just been told by his American friend that his teacher had tried to make life difficult for him but that fortunately "she had nothing on him."

A special type of vocabulary learning problem arises with words that are very similar in the foreign and native languages, but that nevertheless have different meanings and usages. There are many words that appear in similar form in English and the various languages of Europe, either because they borrowed them from each other or from Latin or because they have a common derivation. In many cases these words are used with very similar or identical meanings and in fact facilitate the speaking and comprehension of, let us say, French or Spanish for the native speaker of English. Yet in many cases the similarity between the English word and the foreign word is accidental, or the meanings have changed to the point where the similarity is a hindrance rather than a help: French **librairie** (Spanish **librería**) is used for *bookstore;* French **assister** (Spanish **asistir**) is usually used with the meaning *to be present;* French **conferénce** (Spanish **conferencia**) means *lecture;* and French **lecture** (Spanish **lectura**) means *reading.*

Another series of problems is created because different languages will, so to speak, subdivide different concepts or activities differently. Some languages will introduce subdivisions and distinctions where other languages do not see the necessity of making any distinction whatsoever. As a native speaker of English you may perhaps wonder why German, French, or Spanish need two words for the concept of *know*, why Spanish needs two words for the concept of *be*, French two words for the concept of *day* (and two for *evening*), etc. Yet you take for granted the existence of (and distinction between) *say*, *speak*, *talk*, and *tell*, all of which—at least from the point of view of many languages—seem to describe the same sort of activity. And you are probably not particularly bothered by the fact that in the sentence *I can do this in one hour*, *in* is utterly ambiguous because it can imply *an hour from now*, or *it will take me one hour to do this*. Yet in translating the sentence into French you would have to make an obligatory commitment as to which meaning of *in* you had in mind.

In considering the whole problem of meaning of words, it is also important to realize that languages function in a specific cultural environment. Their words are used to refer to objects, concepts, and ideas that exist in that environment. If these objects or concepts have no counterparts in the culture of the learner, then he must get to know the cultural environment of the foreign language in order to understand the real meaning of the words that he is learning. A Frenchman equating the American *drugstore* with the French dictionary equivalent **pharmacie** has a very wrong concept if he assumes that they refer to the same type of establishment (in a **pharmacie** you buy medicine or toilet articles not ice cream sodas, hardware, or magazines). With more abstract concepts, the cultural and environmental differences may cause more subtle, but perhaps even more important, problems in establishing the exact meaning of words. The dictionary equivalents of words like *freedom*, *democracy*, *liberty*, etc., do not tell us that the very concepts themselves may have different meanings for different cultures.

Learning Exercises

1. Rewrite the following sentences in English using as few words as possible of the original sentence:

   1. I had some trouble getting out of the country.

2. Charles can make himself understood in French.

3. I ordered him to write this letter.

Sample Answer: 1. Leaving the country was quite difficult for me. 2. Charles is getting along quite well in French. 3. I had him pen this letter.

2. The following English sentences are approximate equivalents of each other. Give examples of sentences in which "word equation" established on the basis of these sentences would *not* hold true:

1. I don't get the meaning of this. = I don't understand the meaning of this.

2. He has about two million dollars. = He has approximately two million dollars.

3. Robert started the fight. = Robert began the fight.

4. He gathered the flowers in a basket. = He collected the flowers in a basket.

5. I feel that you are right. = I think that you are right.

Sample Answer: 1. I didn't get the money. 2. He is talking about my friend. 3. Robert started the motor. 4. I gather that you are right. 5. I feel sick.

3. The following are actually sentences produced by nonnatives learning English. See whether you can identify in each case the specific reason for the vocabulary mistake.

1. My friend has two sons, Mary and John.

2. I say you the truth.

3. In this class it gives lots of fun.

4. He arrived at Saturday at eight.

Answer: 1. The native language (Spanish) does not have a word corresponding to the English word *children*, indicating filial relationship without implying the sex of the child. 2. The native language (French) normally uses the same word for both English *say* and *tell*. 3. The individual (whose native language is German) has translated an idiom literally. The German idiom for *there is*, *there are* is literally "it gives" (**es gibt**). 4. Since *at* is used to indicate location in time with hours (*at eight o'clock*), why shouldn't it be used with days (*Saturday*)?

4. The following vocabulary mistakes (made by a speaker of French) are all due to the deceptive similarity of certain English and French words. In each case indicate the English word that the learner meant to use:

1. I had looked forward to the event all day. You can imagine my *deception* when my parents *defended* me to go there.
2. When I asked him to lend me the book, he told me that I could *guard* it for two days.
3. Robert just loves modern painting. He is a real *amateur*.
4. The noise became so loud that I could not *support* it any longer.
5. You must be very careful with what you say to Charlotte. She is very *sensible*.

Answer: 1. disappointment, forbade (did not allow)   2. keep
3. lover (fan, connoisseur)   4. stand   5. sensitive

10

Problems in Syntax:

Confusion of Patterns

Different languages may use different methods to express structural relationships and to express the grammatical meaning of a sentence. English relies heavily on word order, to some extent on function words, and only to a very limited extent on grammatical endings. The -*s* endings of the noun plural and of the third person singular of the verb (and their variants) are today some of the chief remnants of a once much more refined and elaborate system of endings. In other languages the situation is very different: Latin relies almost exclusively on endings to express the relationships and meanings for which English uses word order or function words. Russian and German also rely much more heavily on endings than English. To repeat and give more examples: the subject-object relationship, which in English is expressed by word order alone (*The boy sees the father; the father sees the boy*), is expressed in both Latin and German by endings: **Puer videt patrem; Patrem videt puer** both mean *The boy sees the father;* so do **Der Vater sieht den Knaben** and **Den Knaben sieht der Vater.** The switch in word order does not affect the meaning of the sentence at all: it is used only for emphasis or stylistic effect. Only a change in the endings would affect the grammatical meanings. Languages that rely very heavily on media different from those utilized in the native language are generally considered very difficult. In actual practice, the language often turns out to be no more difficult than others—and for some people at least they are, as a matter of fact, easier than languages whose syntactical media are closer to those of the native tongue. The simple reason for this is that similarity to the native tongue may be a help in one respect but may also increase the possibility of confusion and mix-up.

In no area of language is it more obvious than in syntax that the main enemy of correct foreign language learning is simply confusion —usually not random confusion, but patterned, "organized" confusion, due to the predictable interference of one language system with another.

The most common mistake is simply the assembling of words according to the blueprints of the native language rather than according to those of the language to be learned. From the following examples—all mistakes made in English by speakers of foreign languages—you can almost guess the patterning required by their native languages.

Example 1

The native language puts the object pronouns before the verb (French):

I him see.　　I them know very well.

Example 2

The verb of the subordinate clause is normally in final position (German):

Karl cannot come because he sick is.
Robert explained this so that Karl his problem understands.
He studies hard because his parents ambitious are.

Example 3

The possessive adjective agrees in number and gender with the noun it modifies; it does not agree with the possessor (French):

Charles and John like her house (for "their house").
I did not receive hers letters (for "his letters").

Note that the French words for "house" and "letter" are of the feminine gender.

Example 4

The past participle of a compound verb form is put at the end of the sentence (German):

Charles has with his two brothers arrived.
Robert has me always difficulties made.
Karl had the pictures painted.

Note that the last sentence is perfectly good English, but it does not express what the speaker meant to say, namely *Karl had painted the pictures*. In a language like English in which word order is significant, any mix-up in the word order may produce a sentence with a different meaning.

Example 5

Infinitives are used after prepositions (Spanish, German, or French):

Without to work we cannot succeed.
Before to leave I want to tell you the truth.

Example 6

The future is used in a subordinate clause if the action described takes place in the future (French):

When he will come I will speak to him.
As soon as he will arrive, please let me know.

A very frequent source of mistakes lies in the misapplication of a pattern that by itself is perfectly possible but simply does not fit into the situation. A very common error of this type is the use of wrong tenses. Different languages "cut up" time according to different patterns. The way in which English considers time may seem strange to the speaker of the foreign language. To give three examples:

Example 1

English distinguishes a "progressive" tense, *I am working*, from a simple form, *I work*. In a sense, only the form *I am working* is a genuine present; e.g., to the question *What are you doing right now?* you might say *I am working* (namely, at this very moment). But a statement like *I work at Macy's* does not really refer to a present activity taking place at the moment at which the statement is made. It means that you work there regularly—yesterday, today, and probably tomorrow—while at the moment you make the statement you may be sitting at the dinner table. We might say that a statement like *I work at Macy's* does not refer to any specific time at all. Speakers of languages like German or French have great difficulty distinguishing the use of these two English forms: to a question like *What are you doing right now?* they might answer *I do my homework*, and in turn, to the inquiry *What did you do in Paris last year?* you may get the answer *I was working in a store*.

Example 2

In English the present perfect, *I have spoken*, signifies an action that took place in the past. The exact time at which it took place is not relevant to the speaker. *I have spoken* is a *past indefinite*. Thus you might ask *Have you spoken to Robert?* and the answer would be *Yes, I have spoken to him;* but at the moment in which the *time* at which you spoke to him becomes relevant, you must change the tense: *Oh yes, I SPOKE to him at six o'clock.* French (and to some extent also colloquial German) does not make this distinction. In French a compound tense corresponding to *I have spoken* is used not only to denote the *past indefinite* action, but also the action described by the *past* (spoke) form of English. I have heard many Frenchmen say things like: *Oh yes, I have seen him yesterday at six, but then he has left. Then Charles has come and I have begun to talk to him right away.*

Example 3

We have stated in our discussion of English syntax that any simple form of the verb can be replaced by *have + past participle*. Thus *I work* can be changed to *I have worked*, and *I am working* or *I was working* to *I have been working* or *I had been working*. The meaning of the last two is quite difficult for the speaker of many languages (French, German, Spanish included) to comprehend, for *I have been working* means in fact that you started working some time ago and are still working now. To speakers of languages that lack the English pattern shown by *I have been working*, it seems rather clear that the mere fact that an action is still going on dictates the choice of the present tense: *I study English now for over two years; I travel in the United States since last April*, etc.

Another important source of error lies in misapplying the possible transformations in the foreign language. We have pointed out that most English verbs admit the transformation into the progressive tense: *I work > I am working, I worked > I was working*, etc. The progressive tense can in turn be transformed by replacing the present form of *be* by *have* + past participle of *be: I am working > I have been working*, etc.:

I work > I am working > I have been working
I think > I am thinking > I have been thinking
I laugh > I am laughing > I have been laughing

Yet there are a few verbs with which the first (and with it usually the second) of the above transformations are normally impossible. But a foreigner studying English may be unaware of this and produce these transformations anyway:

I understand his ideas > I am understanding his ideas > I have been understanding his ideas

I know Mr. Smith > I am knowing Mr. Smith > I have been knowing Mr. Smith

I am in New York > I am being in New York > I have been being in New York

Another example of misapplying patterns comes from the so-called two-part verbs that we discussed in Part I. Since in the sentence *I call on Mary, on* functions as a preposition, the pronoun replacement follows the pattern of *I walk with Mary: I walk with her, I call on her.* In the sentence *I call up Mary, call up* is a two-part verb. *Up* functions as a part of the verb and the pronoun replacement follows a different pattern: *I call her up.* To the native speaker this switch in pattern is natural, but to the learner of the language it is bewildering. Let us replace the nouns by pronouns in the following sentences and watch the switch in pattern:

Get on your coat!   Get it on!
Get on your horse!   Get on it!
Get off his coat!   Get off it!
Get his coat off!   Get it off!

(Aside from showing the switch in the pronoun replacement pattern, the above example also gives evidence of the problem created by the various meanings of expressions like *get on, get off, get in, get out, put on, put off, put up*, etc. English is not easy.)

The problem of pattern confusion is usually made worse if the native and foreign languages seem to agree very neatly. Then the foreign language "makes an exception," and the native language does not follow along. In such cases one might say that the native and foreign languages seem to conspire to mislead the student. In many languages (French, German, to some extent Spanish) making a sentence negative involves using a negative particle or expression of negation, and making it interrogative requires a change in word order (like putting the subject after the verb). In English the function words such as *will*, *may*, and *can* follow the pattern:

I may work.	I may not work.	May I work?
I can work.	I cannot work	Can I work?

For the speaker of French or German this is easy; but he may be paying a heavy price, because the very agreement between his language and English may only reinforce his tendency to say:

I work.	I work not.	Work I?
I understand.	I understand not.	Understand I?

Learning Exercises

1. The following contain examples of mistakes due to faulty patterning. In each case identify briefly the probable reason for the error:

   1. I was not knowing any of his friends.
      We are not understanding mathematics at all.

   2. Charles has must to leave.
      Robert will can be with us.

   3. Charles studies medicine for two years.
      Robert studies French for two years now and will continue for two more.

   4. I know the book and I even know to the author.
      I understand his situation, but to him I do not understand at all.

   5. I cannot get along without to speak English.
      He began by to read the examples.

6. He answered without me to look at.
   He worked hard in order his parents to please.

7. I don't like a man whose I don't understand the intentions.
   This is a man whose you know the ideas very well.

8. Charles is gone to the game.
   His letters are not arrived yet.
   I am sorry I am come late.

9. I know exactly what Charles and his friends done have.
   Can you me tell when the performance begin will.

10. I worked for three hours when you have interrupted me.
    I read the paper when the telegram is come.

11. Charles does not have learned his lesson.
    Robert did not can understand me.

12. I can to speak English quite well.
    Carlos must to learn to speak English.

13. Do I can go with you?
    Did I must learn all this?

Answer:

1. Wrong extension of the progressive tense transformation (native language: German).

2. Extension of the use of *auxiliaries* with other function words of that class. Treatment of those function words as if they were normal regular verbs (native language: French).

3. Lack of comprehension of the English *has been* + *-ing* form construction and its replacement by a present or a past perfect (native language: German).

4. Extension of a foreign pattern to English. The native language of the speaker (Spanish) requires a preposition (**a** equated with *to*) before direct objects if they represent persons (but not if they represent things).

5. The native language (French) requires the infinitive after prepositions.

6. The native language (German) requires the infinitive after prepositions and puts the infinitive after the object.

7. In the relative clause English places the object modified by

   whose before the subject: *I know the daughter*, but *a man whose*

   daughter I know. The native language of the speaker (French) does not follow this feature of English.

8. With certain verbs (such as *go, come, arrive*) the native language (French) uses the normal equivalent of the verb *to be* (rather than *have*) to form a past indefinite tense.

9. The native language (German) puts the auxiliary verb at the end of the subordinate clause.

10. The native language (French) has no progressive tense.

11. The native language of the speaker (German) probably had nothing to do with this mistake. He overextended the normal English negation pattern (don't, doesn't, didn't) to the auxiliaries.

12. This mistake is due partly to the native language (Spanish) and partly to a misunderstanding of English structure. In English the simple form of the verb is normally linked to a preceding verb by the word *to*. This *to* can be considered as a morpheme necessitated by the construction. After the function words (*can, will, may, must*, etc.) English does not use the *to: I begin to write, I try to write*, etc., but *I can write, I must write*. In Spanish the form required after another verb is the infinitive. Having equated *to write* with the infinitive of his language, the student is using it also after the English auxiliaries, and thus wrongly extending a pattern of English as well as superimposing a pattern of Spanish.

13. The source of error is the same as in number 11 above. A pattern of English (this time the interrogative pattern with *do, does, did*) has been wrongly extended to the auxiliary verbs.

IV

How to Learn a Foreign Language

11

Learning

the Sound System

In the area of pronunciation—more than in any other aspect of language—it is most obvious that understanding and good advice alone will never take the place of a good mixture of ability and, above all, practice. The author of this book knows several linguists and phoneticians who speak foreign languages with a considerable foreign accent, and many students who—without any understanding of phonetic or phonemic problems—managed to acquire native or at least near-native pronunciations. Nevertheless, an understanding of just what abilities are involved and what kind of practice it takes will prove helpful. Having an *acceptable* pronunciation in a foreign language means that you can pronounce the sounds in the foreign language in such a way that a native speaker recognizes and can hear the differences between them. Having a *good* pronunciation implies that you actually pronounce the foreign sounds as they are produced by the native speaker and that you do not substitute the sounds of your own language. This means that pronouncing correctly implies an ability to *hear* correctly: You must hear (1) the differences among the foreign speech sounds and (2) the differences between them and the sounds of your own language that you are likely to substitute.

This ability to *hear correctly* does not automatically assure that you pronounce correctly, but it is almost inevitably a *prerequisite.* For if you cannot *hear* a sound correctly, you cannot imitate it correctly, and the effort to imitate and practice that sound will be largely wasted. Furthermore, if you cannot hear whether or not you are pronouncing a word correctly, practice alone will not do very much good, because you won't know whether you are practicing a right or a wrong pronunciation. An analogy with music will help illustrate this point: having a "good ear" does not make you a good musician, but having a "bad ear" will keep you from becoming one. Hours and hours of practicing an instrument will not produce a virtuoso if the student is incapable of telling a wrong note from a right one.

Most language teachers thus believe that all students, but especially those whom nature has not endowed with a "good ear for languages," are in need of ear training. Typically, this ear training takes the form of practice in listening and recognizing those sound differences that we have just mentioned: namely, the differences among the phonemes of the foreign language and the differences between the foreign phonemes and those native ones that are unacceptable and obnoxious substitutes. To give a few examples: a foreign student learning English may have only one high front vowel phoneme and one high back vowel phoneme in this native system. Before teaching him to pronounce the English /i/, /ɪ/ and the /u/, /ʊ/ phonemes, we will first expose him to listening drills in which he learns to hear the contrasts between the two English sounds /i/ and /ɪ/ and the two English sounds /u/ and /ʊ/. Minimal pairs—words distinguished by the critical sounds alone—will serve best for that purpose: *beat/bit, seat/sit, feet/fit, deed/did,* etc. may be used as the basis for an /i/, /ɪ/ listening drill. For /u/ and /ʊ/ we could use *Luke/look, suit/soot, pool/pull,* etc. If the student's difficulty is pronouncing the /s/ and /z/ phonemes of English, the listening drill will take the form of distinguishing between minimal pairs like *racer/razor, seal/zeal, ice/eyes, lacy/lazy,* etc.

If the substitute sound which the student is likely to use is in itself a phoneme of the language to be learned, then the training designed to prevent substitution is of course the same that is involved in combatting confusion of sounds. If you had to train a student who was substituting /s/ for /θ/, you would have him listen to pairs like *sick/thick, sin/thin, sank/thank,* etc. If the substitute sound is *not* a phoneme in the language to be learned, then the whole problem is less serious. If you are satisfied with sounding like a foreigner and having a thick accent, then go ahead and substitute the sounds of your native language. This is exactly the advice which—by necessity—is found in manuals for travellers, soldiers, etc., in which the sounds of the foreign language are transcribed in terms of native language equivalents. Thus French **les livres** may be transcribed as *lay leever* and the reader of the manual told to pronounce the words that way. If, however, your goal is to really learn the foreign language, then you must exactly reverse the procedure of the travel handbooks. In other words, you must learn to hear the difference between *lay leever* and what the French really say—and then pronounce the words in the French, *not* in the American way. Ear training then takes the form of contrasting the foreign speech sounds with the native substitutes. This can be done by contrasting the sounds in isolation, in syllables, or by contrasting words of the two languages—especially if the two words sound nearly alike, except for precisely the difference involved in their being words of different languages: a pair like the one just mentioned, French **les,** English *lay,* is a good example of the type of minimal pair that can be used to sharpen the ear to differences between sounds of different languages.

Even if you can hear the difference between the phonemes of the foreign language and the distinction between foreign sounds and those of your native language, you cannot necessarily imitate the sounds correctly. In such cases, an "articulatory recipe"—a description of how to produce the sound—can be of tremendous help. Good books and good teachers will usually be able to supply good articulatory recipes for the sounds of foreign languages. Here the pupil and teacher must both keep in mind that advice on how to say a particular sound should be short, clear, precise, and unambiguous. Unless the articulatory description tells you exactly what to do with your speech organs, it is probably of very little value. The best advice usually tells you to start with a familiar sound of your own language, and then specifies in precise terms how to introduce a modification that will lead to the foreign sound. Thus a Frenchman or a Spaniard normally says his /t/ sound with the tip of the tongue against the teeth. In telling him how to produce the English /t/

sound, you would have to point out that he sould put the tip of his
tongue farther back in the mouth against the alveolar ridge. Frenchmen or Spaniards have no /ŋ/ phoneme. In teaching them how to
say the /ŋ/ sound as in *rung*, *sang*, etc., you would start by having
them say *rug*, *sag*, with the familiar /g/ sound, and then ask them
to modify the sound by maintaining the closure at the contact point
of the tongue against the velum and making a humming sound.
On the other hand, advice such as "say the sound more softly,"
"make a sort of hushing noise," or "produce the sound very distinctly," usually means only that the teacher or the textbook was
not too sure of what to say.

Distinct from—but at the same time intimately connected with—
genuine pronunciation problems are those created by orthography
and orthographic interference. Languages like English, in which
various sounds are represented by the same orthographic symbols
and the same sound by a variety of symbols, will obviously cause
difficulties. When it comes to lack of consistency in sound-symbol
relationship, English is one of the worst languages. If a certain sound
is represented by a specific symbol or symbols in the native language,
and the same symbol or symbols are used to represent a different
sound in the foreign language, we have, as we have mentioned
already, an additional source of error and confusion. In order to
avoid confusion and interference coming from orthography, many
language teachers will avoid the use of writing in the initial stages
of instruction. They will introduce spelling and writing only *after*
the pupil has had a chance to develop correct pronunciation. If
you happen to be a person who is strongly "visually minded"—in
other words one who needs the support of visual aids or symbols to
reinforce his memory—you may find this procedure disconcerting,
although it is probably for your ultimate benefit. At any rate, sooner
or later the visual orthographic symbols for the speech sounds must
be introduced. Eventually you must learn in the foreign language
the connections among sounds and symbols and the spelling patterns, just as you had to learn them in your own language. In
connection with this, it should also be pointed out that foreign
languages which use nonalphabetic writing systems (Chinese) or
alphabets different from that of the native language (Russian,
Greek, etc.) may initially be somewhat difficult, but often turn out
to offer fewer pronunciation or spelling pronunciation problems,

because there is no interference coming from already established sound-symbol associations.

If you were to teach English to a nonnative, you would sooner or later have to establish the knowledge of the fact that the phoneme /i/ is related to the spellings *ie* (*believe, grief*), *ei* (*receive, either, deceive*), *ea* (*bead, mean*), *ee* (*greet, speed*), *e* (*me, she*), etc. And, to give one more example, your pupil would sooner or later have to realize that the sound /e/ may be written *ea* (*great*), *ai* (*vain, rain*), *ay* (*say, play*), *ei* (*vein, reindeer*), *a* (*mane, fate*), etc. In a systematic way this knowledge could probably be established most easily by having your pupil write series of words in which the /i/ and /e/ sounds appear with different spellings and series of words in which the sounds are consistently spelled in the same way. In addition, your pupil would have to learn to realize the spelling patterns of English, e.g., the addition of a final -*e* in orthography usually means a change from /æ/ to /e/ in the stem vowel, *man/mane, Dan/Dane, fat/fate*. The same addition of -*e* also usually implies a change from /ɪ/ to /aɪ/: *bit/bite, spit/spite*, or /ə/ to /(y)u/: *cut/cute, tub/tube*, etc. If a single symbol or combination of symbols is already associated with a sound of the native language, special reading practice may be called for. The Frenchman who has learned through his native language to react with the sound /ʃ/ (*SHe*) to the letters *ch* may need reading drills in pronouncing /č/ in *Charles, chin, church, much*, etc.

Learning Exercises and Questions

1. Imagine that you are a teacher of English as a foreign language. How would you devise auditory discrimination exercises for the following problems?

   1. Your pupils' native language has only two front vowel phonemes, /e/ and /i/.
   2. Their language has the sound /č/ (*CHin*), but not the sound /ĵ/ (*Gin*).
   3. The native language of your pupils does not distinguish between /b/ and /p/: the sound /p/ appears initially and in final position, and /b/ between vowels.

   Answer: 1. Contrast minimal pairs like *bet/bait, let/late*, *pen/pain, led/laid, wet/wait; bean/bin, heap/hip, leak/lick, deed/ did*, etc. 2. Contrast pairs like *chin/gin, cheap/jeep, chew/Jew, rich/ridge, batch/badge*, etc. 3. Contrast pairs like *bin/pin, bay/pay, bee/pea, nap/nab, rip/rib, tapping/tabbing, ripping/rib-bing, clapper/clabber*, etc.

2. Devise "articulatory recipes" for the following situations:

   1. The foreign language does not have the sound /f/.

   2. The foreign language does not have the sound /θ/; it does have the dental sounds /s/ and /t/.

   3. The foreign language has sounds similar to /ɔ/ (*bOUght*) and /a/ (*hOt*); it does not have the sound /ə/ (*bUt*).

Answer:

   1. Study how you produce the sound, then describe it ex-actly: put the upper teeth against the lower lip, and force the airstream through the obstacle thus created. Say *fin, fast, feet, father*, etc.

   2. The main difference between a dental /s/ and the /θ/ sound is that in the /θ/ sound of *thin, thick*, etc. the tip of the tongue is not grooved and rests against the upper teeth. In order to avoid the grooving, you could tell your pupil to put the tip of his tongue *between* his teeth when saying the sound.

   3. Tell your pupil to say *bought* first. Have him observe that for the vowel sound in *bought* and *ought* the lips are rounded. Then have him say the word again but with his lips unrounded while he is saying the vowel. If neces-sary, have him say the vowel with spread lips. (This will give a sound that is closer to the British pronunciation than the American one, but still distinct from *bought*.) Another possibility is to start with the /a/ sound of *hot*, and have the student close his jaw somewhat (thus raising the tongue) to arrive at the /ə/ sound.

3. What spelling and reading exercises would you introduce if the foreign language required:

1. The pronunciation /č/ (*CH*air) for *c* before *i* and *e*.
2. The pronunciation /aɪ/ (*lIke*) for the spelling *ei*.
3. The pronunciation /u/ for the spelling *ou*.

Answer: 1. Dictation and reading of words like *cents, receive, ceiling,* etc. 2. Dictation and reading of words like *receive, deceive,* etc., and, to counteract the native spelling habit, a series like *site, spite, bite, like,* etc. 3. Dictation and reading of the common spellings of /u/ in English, e.g., *food, mood, rude, nude,* etc., and, to counteract the native pattern, a series like *house, foul, mouth,* etc.

The following exercises may be answered with examples of any foreign language that you have studied or are studying. Sample answers will be provided for French, Spanish, and German.

4. Make a complete list of all the vowel sounds of the foreign language. Give at least one word as an example for each sound. (Keep in mind that the purpose of this exercise is to help you systematize your knowledge of the foreign language, *not* to teach it).

Answer:

French: French has the following vowels (symbols are those conventionally used in most textbooks):

/i/ **lire, si**	/y/ **mur**	/u/ **doux**
/e/ **les, j'ai**	/ø/ **deux**	/o/ **beau, dos, faut**
/ɛ/ **même, dette**	/œ/ **peur**	/ɔ/ **botte**
/a/ **car**	/ə/ **le**	/ɑ/ **bas**

In addition, French has four nasal vowels:

/ã/ **dans**   /ɔ̃/ **bon**   /œ̃/ **un**   /ɛ̃/ **vin**

Spanish: The Spanish vowel system is extremely simple. There are only five significant vowel units:

/i/ **ira**	/u/ **escucho, burro**
/e/ **se, perro**	/o/ **rojo, donde**
	/a/ **dar**

German: The vowel sounds of German are:

/i/ **sie, ihn**	/ö/ **Götter**
/ɪ/ **bitte, irren**	/u/ **Ruhm, Mut**

/e/ sehen, Weh	/ü/ zum, Butter,
/ɛ/ wetten, wenn	/o/ Bohne, Sohn
/ü/ fühle, kühn	/ɔ/ voll, Gott
/ü/ Mütter, füttern	/ɑ/ Wahn, Rat
/ö/ Söhne, Goethe	/a/ Ratte, wann

In addition, German also has a very open sound as in **Bär, spät,** the umlaut **ä,** which some Germans keep distinct from the /e/ phoneme, especially in reading aloud and careful pronunciation. Many Germans, however, do not distinguish these two sounds, and they pronounce words like **Meere** (*oceans*) and **Mähre** (*old horse*) the same way. In unaccented position alone, German has furthermore the vowel /ə/ **sagən, arbeitətə.**

The diphthongs of German are:

/aɪ/ **mein, drei**   /ɔɪ/ **Leute, Häuser**
/aʊ/ **Haus, bauen**

5. Compare the list of vowels of the foreign language with the list of the English vowels given in Part I of this book. On the basis of your comparison, decide which of the vowels of the foreign language are difficult to distinguish. For each difficulty give at least one pair of words (preferably a "minimal pair") to illustrate the problem.

Answer:

French: The main problems in auditory discrimination are
1. Hearing the distinction between the nasal vowels:

/ã/, /ɔ̃/ **dans/dont, vent/vont**
/ã/, /œ̃/ **l'an/l'un**
/ɛ̃/, /œ̃/ **lin/l'un**

Fortunately, many Frenchmen are dropping the distinction between /ɛ̃/ and /œ̃/ (**lin/l'un**) in their speech, probably because it is a distinction that is utilized very little in the language.

2. The distinction between the vowels /o/ and /ø/ (**dos/deux**), /u/ and /y/ (**doux/du, roue/rue**) are also quite troublesome.

3. The distinction between /a/ and /ɑ/ (**car**/**bas**) is of little use in the language and is being dropped by some Frenchmen.

4. One distinction which is troublesome for some students will not become clear from the comparison of the vowel charts alone: In English, vowels before nasal consonants are often slightly nasalized (*down, ample*). In French they are normally not nasalized before a pronounced nasal consonant, and they are kept distinct from nasal vowels. Thus **Jeanne** is pronounced with a nonnasal vowel (followed by **n**), **Jean** is pronounced with a nasal vowel (but the **n** after the vowel is not pronounced). As a speaker of English you must be watchful of this distinction when pronouncing **bon**/**bonne**, **an**/**Anne**, **son**/**sonne**, etc.

Spanish: As a speaker of English you should have very little discrimination difficulty in Spanish. The only real problem may occur in the unaccented syllable where English often loses the vowel distinctions and uses the /ə/ sound (*sofA*). As a result of this English habit, you may fail to distinguish (in hearing and speech) between unaccented vowels: **am**o/**am**a, **com**o/**com**a/**com**e, **habl**o/**habl**e. (Remember that even worse than *not* making the distinction would be to shift the accent or stress in order to make it. Then you will be most certainly incomprehensible, since stress is a phoneme of Spanish and by shifting the stress you may change the meaning.)

German: Since so many of the English and German vowel phonemes are so similar, the English-speaking student should have little difficulty in hearing the distinctions among the German vowels. The only possible problem areas are:

1. The distinctions in pronunciation between /u/ and /ü/ (**Blut**/**Blüte**), and /o/ and /ö/ (**Sohn**/**Söhne**); the distinction in both pronunciation and discrimination between /i/ and /ü/ (**Tiere**/**Türe**), /e/ and /ö/ (**Sehne**/**Söhne**).

2. A very troublesome vowel distinction not revealed by the phonemic chart is the one between the vowel /ə/ (**bitte**) and the usual German pronunciation of **-er** at the end of

the word. Here German does not use an *r-like* pronunciation at all, but the variant of /r/ which is used in this
position is really a vowel, very much like the /ə/ in **bitte**,
but with the tongue slightly more drawn back. Since
English has only one /ə/ sound (which admits a great
range of variants), you may, as a native speaker of English, have a problem in hearing the distinction between
bitte/bitter, Wette/Wetter, etc.

6. Does the foreign language have any vowel sounds that are
   so different from English that as a native speaker of English
   you do not have *any* acceptable (in the sense of comprehensible) substitute sounds?

Answer:

French: Yes. The sounds /y/ (**du**), /ø/ (**deux**), /œ/ (**peur**),
and the nasal sounds /ã/ (**dans**), /ɔ̃/ (**dont**), /œ̃/ (**un**),
/ɛ̃/ (**vin**) have no near counterparts that could be used
without disturbing clarity of communication.

Spanish: No. Note that the vowel system of Spanish is quite
simple and that you have a great deal of latitude in making
substitutions. Your English vowels would not sound very
good, but they would probably be understood.

German: Yes. English has no acceptable (readily comprehensible) counterparts of /ü/ (**Tür**), /ü/ (**Hütte**), /ö/
(**Söhne**), /ɔ̃/ (**Götter**).

7. Which of the English vowel sounds that are likely to be used
   as substitute sounds by an English speaker are the least acceptable to the native speaker and are the most obvious and
   objectionable mark of a strong English accent?

Answer:

French: The substitution of the strongly diphthongal English
/i/, /e/, /u/, /o/ sounds (*see, say, doe, do*) for their French
counterparts (**si, ses, dos, doux**). If you want to get rid
of this feature of English accent in French, be sure that

you can *hear* and *make* the distinction between English and French pairs like the ones just mentioned. To give further examples (English word given first, French second): *may*/**mes,** *lay*/**les,** *fee*/**fit,** *lee*/**lit,** *so*/**sot,** *low*/**l'eau,** *sue*/**sous,** *coo*/**coup,** etc.

Spanish: Substitution of the English diphthongal /i/, /e/, /u/, /o/ sounds for their nondiphthongal Spanish counterparts: Spanish **mi, se** pronounced like English *me, say,* Spanish **muro** with the vowel of English *do,* or **toro** with the vowel of *tone.*

German: Substitution of the English diphthongal vowels /i/, /e/, /u/, /o/ for their German nondiphthongal counterparts. In other words, the substitution of the vowels of English *sea, gay, bone, mood* in German **sie, geh, Bohne, Mut.** Since English /ɔ/—depending on the dialect—is also produced with variants, glides, and is lengthened, it is not a very good substitute for German /ɔ/: **Gott** should not have the same vowel sound as *bought.*

8. Does the foreign language have any consonant sounds for which English does not provide an acceptable (comprehensible) substitute?

Answer:

French: Not really. If you classify the second sound produced in **lui** /ɥ/ (which is really a semivowel) among the consonants, then this sound would have no direct counterpart in English. The French phoneme /ɲ/ as in **agneau** has no counterpart in the English sound system, but the English combination /n/ + /y/ (*onion*) is a comprehensible substitute.

Spanish: Spanish has a phoneme /ɲ/ **(año),** and—in some dialects at least—/ʎ/ **(ella).** English has neither, but the combination /n/ + /y/ of English *onion* is an acceptable substitute for /ɲ/, and most English speakers can pronounce the combination /l/ + /y/ to substitute for /ʎ/. The sounds of Spanish for which English provides no substitutes whatever are /x/ **(jefe, general),** the trilled

/ʀ/ (**perro**)—which, if an English /r/ is simply substituted is likely to merge with the flap /r/ of **pero**—and the
sounds used for the pronunciation of orthographic *b* and
g between vowels: /β/ (**lobo**), and /ɣ/ (**lago**). For the
pronunciation of intervocalic *d*, English does have a substitute: /ð/ in Spanish **lado** has approximately the same
sound as English /ð/ in *father*. However, many speakers of
English will substitute /d/, under the influence of Spanish
orthography. As far as the sound /ʀ/ (**perro**) is concerned, remember that it is produced by vibration of the
tip of the tongue against the alveolar ridge. The /x/ of
jefe is a continuant produced at approximately the same
point of articulation as /k/ in *could:* Say /k/, then release
the obstacle slowly while continuing to say the sound.
The /ɣ/ of **lago** is produced at the same point of articulation as /g/ but is also a continuant: Say /g/ and release
the obstacle slightly so that air can come through during
sound production. The /β/ of **lobo** is also a continuant
produced at exactly the same point of articulation as /b/:
Say /b/ and then release the obstacle slightly so that the
air can go through between the lips as you are saying the
sound.

German: English has no phonemes that are counterparts of
the German "affricates" /pf/ (**Pfeife**) and /ts/ (**zu**). The
English combination of /t/ + /s/ (*cats*) is a good substitute for the German /ts/, and English speakers have no
problem combining /p/ and /f/ as in *campfire*. The real
problem consonant sounds are /ç/ and /x/—usually referred to as the **ich** and **ach** Laute. They are continuants
produced at the point of articulation of /k/ in *kin* and
could. Say /k/ as in *sick* or *lack* and try to release the
obstacle slightly so that air can go through during the
pronunciation of the sound; this will approximate /x/.
For the **ich** sound, you can try to pronounce /y/ of
English *yes* and German **ja,** and see whether, while maintaining the same position but using no voice, you can
force air through the narrow aperture to produce the
sound /ç/.

9. Which of the substitute consonant sounds likely to be used by a speaker of English are the least acceptable, in the sense that they are the most obvious mark of a strong English accent?

Sample Answer:

French: The most objectionable substitutes are:

1. The English /r/. English /r/ is a retroflex (see p. 24) and a semi vowel. The standard French /r/ is a voiced continuant produced at approximately the same point of articulation as the consonant /g/ (say /g/ as in *go* and try to relax the obstacle so that the air can come through during the production of the sound).

2. English /p/, /t/, /k/. French /p/, /t/, /k/—unlike their English counterparts—are always unaspirated and are fully articulated also at the end of the word. French /t/ is dental (tip of tongue against teeth), not an alveolar (tip of tongue against alveolar ridge).

3. English /l/ (usually pronounced as an alveolar sound— tip of the tongue against the alveolar ridge—or as a velar—back of the tongue raised toward the velum). The French /l/ is a dental (tip of the tongue against the teeth). Compare French **belle** with English *bell*.

Spanish: The objectionable substitutes are:

1. English /r/. Spanish /r/ is not a semi vowel but a sound produced by flapping the tip of the tongue against the alveolar ridge. Actually the *d* of English *ladder* is a much better and closer substitute for Spanish /r/ than English /r/.

2. Spanish /l/ is a dental (tip of the tongue against the teeth), while English /l/ is an alveolar (tip of tongue against alveolar ridge) or velar (back of tongue drawn toward the velum).

3. English aspirated /p/, /t/, /k/, because Spanish /p/, /t/, /k/ are always unaspirated. Spanish /t/ is a dental, not an alveolar.

German: The most irritating substitutes are:

1. English /r/, which is usually a retroflex (see p. 24) and a semivowel. The most commonly used German /r/ is a "vibrant" produced with vibration of the uvula against the back of the tongue. The German /r/ in word (or syllable) final position is a vowel, somewhat like the /ə/ of English *sofa*, but produced with the tongue slightly farther back and with lips slightly spread.

2. The English /l/ sound, which is usually produced as a velarized /l/ (with the back of the tongue raised toward the velum). In the German /l/ the tip of the tongue must make contact against the teeth or the alveolar ridge, while the back of the tongue is kept flat.

10. What are the main intonation problems (stress, pitch, juncture) in the foreign language as far as a native speaker of English is concerned?

Answer:

French: Of all the commonly taught languages, French is probably the most different from English from the standpoint of intonation. The difficulties manifest themselves in comprehension as well as speaking. In the main they consist of the following: (1) English has a phonemic stress accent (Remember: *díscus, discúss*, etc.). French has *no* stress accent. The result is that all syllables of the word have about equal length and stress (only the last syllable of the word or word group is somewhat lengthened). For a speaker of English it is very difficult to say words like **liberté, accident, philosophie** without stressing one syllable more than the others and without shortening or swallowing some syllables. (2) French has, for all practical purposes at least, no special junctures of the English type to mark word boundaries. It is spoken not in words but rather in syllables that tend to end in vowels. Thus the syllabification of **nous avons** is **nou-sa-vons**—phonetically [nu za vɔ̃]. **Il est arrivé** is **i-le(s)-ta-rri-vé**—phonetically [i lɛ ta ri ve]. The result is a major speaking and comprehension problem.

Spanish: The main problem for the speaker of English is the carryover into Spanish of the reduction of vowel distinction in unstressed syllables. Spanish distinguishes only between stressed and unstressed syllables and maintains all vowel distinctions in unstressed as well as stressed syllables. Thus a speaker of English is likely to blur vowel contrasts in the unaccented syllables and to introduce further stress distinctions (secondary, tertiary) where Spanish has none: Spanish **ĕmbărcadérŏ** (only one stress, all other syllables equally unstressed) pronounced as **ĕmbàrcădérŏ**, or even worse, **ɔ̆mbàrkédɔ̆rə**.

German: The German intonation and stress pattern is in many ways very much like English. One of the problems is that German maintains practically all vowel distinctions in unaccented position while English does not. Thus words like **Mathematik, Geographie, Democratie** may be mispronounced by a native speaker of English for two reasons: (1) the stress accent does not fall on the same syllable as in English and (2) the vowel in the unaccented syllables may become blurred, /ə/ rather than the clear *a, e, i, o, u* sounds required by German. German words like **Königin** (*queen*) and **Königen** [*to* (*the*) *kings*] may sound alike as the result of such mispronunciation.

11. Does the foreign language have phonemes that are represented by more than one orthographic symbol? What are some of the most important examples of such inconsistency in the presentation of the sounds?

Answer:

French: Indeed yes. Representation of sounds by orthography is not at all consistent in French (although the situation is not so bad as in English). To give a few of the most important examples:

/e/	**e**ssai, parl**é**, parl**e**r, parl**ai**, n**ei**ger
/ɛ/	d**e**tte, **é**l**è**ve, b**ê**te, n**ei**ge, ma**î**tre
/a/	p**a**rle, f**e**mme
/ɔ/	b**o**tte, **Pau**l

/o/   dos, faut, beau
/ɑ̃/   en, an
/ɛ̃/   vin, vain, sein, vient, faim, simple
/k/   car, quand
/s/   sent, cent, français
/ʒ/   jeu, général
/z/   rose, zéro
/j/   bien, travail, fille, yeux
/g/   gant, guerre

Spanish: Spanish orthography is far more regular than English. There are comparatively few sounds that are represented by more than one symbol. The most important examples are:

/b/   bueno, vino (/β/ lobo, cava)
/g/   gordo, guerra (/ɣ/ daga, azogue)
/k/   cava, que, kilo
/θ/   dice, caza (in Castilian)
/x/   jota, general
/w/   cuatro, huerta
/y/   yo, hierro (non-Castilian: ella)
/s/   (in most varieties) dice, caza, casa

German: German spelling is fairly consistent, certainly more so than English.

Note that (1) doubling of consonant symbols is used to indicate that the preceding vowel is "short" (/ɪ/, /ɛ/, /ʊ/, /ɔ/, /a/) and (2) that in German all final consonants are pronounced as unvoiced. This means (1) that /p/, /t/, /k/ will often be spelled as *pp*, *tt*, *ck* (rather than *kk*) to indicate that the preceding vowel is "short," and (2) that the sounds /p/, /t/, /k/ may be spelled *b*, *d*, *g* at the end of the word. Thus the italicized symbols are all representations of the sound /t/: **Tag, Mitte, Rad.**

The so-called "long" vowels (/i/, /e/, /u/, /o/, /ɑ/) are often represented as a vowel + **h**: *ihm, fehlen, ohne, Huhn.* In the case of /i/ the orthography *ie* (**sie**) is also used. There are also a few words in which the "long" vowels are represented either by a doubling of the symbol (**leer**, *empty;* **Boot**, *boat*) or simply through the fact that the following consonant symbol is not doubled (**tun**, *to do*).

Thus several symbols may be used to represent:

/i/   ih́n, sie
/o/   oh́ne, Boot, Not
/e/   léer, leh́ren, Gebet

Other sounds that may be represented by a variety of symbols are:

/aɪ/   beide, Kaiser
/ɔɪ/   heute, Häute
/ts/   zum, Katze, Nation
/ʃ/   schon, Stein
/s/   das, Wasser, Masse, Maβe (the β symbol is used to indicate /s/ after "long" vowels, since doubling of the *s* symbol is reserved to indicate /s/ after "short" vowels).
/f/   Vater, fahren

12. Does the foreign language utilize symbols or groups of symbols that a native speaker of English is likely to mispronounce because they are used to represent quite different sounds in English?

Answer:

French: Yes, there are several:

qu	used for	/k/	in French	quand	—compare English	*quail*
ti	"	/s/	"	nation	"	*nation*
x	"	/s/	"	dix	"	*Dixie*
l	"	/j/	"	travail	"	*travail*
g	"	/ʒ/	"	général	"	*general*
ch	"	/ʃ/	"	cher	"	*chair*
gn	"	/ɲ/	"	agneau	"	*Agnes*
ai	"	/e/	"	j'ai, vaine	"	*vain*
ou	"	/u/	"	doux	"	*soul, house*
h	no sound value in French			homme	"	*have*

Further note that in French, *n*, *m*, if word final or before another consonant symbol, are usually employed to indicate the nasal vowel, but are themselves silent: **bon, vin,** etc. Also that French word final consonant symbols (with the exception of *c*, *r*, *f*, *l*: Remember *careful!*) are normally not pronounced; that final consonant symbols are sometimes pronounced if the following word begins with a vowel, and this is especially true if the final consonant serves a "grammatical function" (e.g., the final -*s* indicates the plural). The detailed description of these rules is up to the individual textbook; the exact mastery of the problem is a matter of practice. All in all the problems of French orthography and the interference coming from it are fairly complicated.

Spanish: English orthographic habits may combine with some of the Spanish inconsistencies in spelling to produce various types of errors. Here are some that one must watch out for:

h has no sound value in Spanish (**hombre,** compare English *have*).

-*d*-, -*b*-, -*g*- as in **amado, lobo, lago** should be pronounced as continuants, but may be mispronounced as stops because of their English value as well as the Spanish pronunciation in initial position.

v as in **verde** should be pronounced /b/, not like English *very*.

n before *labials* as in **en Barcelona, invierno** should be pronounced /m/.

ll as in **ella,** pronounced /y/ (except in Castilian, /ʎ/); but not /l/ as in English *jelly*.

s before a voiced consonant should be pronounced /z/: **rasgo.**

German: Responses in terms of English orthography rather than German may lead to mispronunciation in several situations. Here are a few important ones for which you must watch out:

w	used for /v/ in German		**Wasser** **Wein**	—compare English		*water*
v	"	/f/	"	**Vater** **von**	"	*van*
ch	"	/ç//x/	"	**ich, ach**	"	*chin*
s(p)	"		"	**spielen**	"	*spin*
s(t)		/ʃ/		**Stunde**		*stand*
I	"	/ts/	"	**zu**	"	*zeal*
qu	"	/kv/	"	**Quelle**	"	*quail*
ti	"	/ts/	"	**Nation**	"	*nation*
kn	"	/kn/	"	**Knochen**	"	*knife*
ei	"	/aɪ/	"	**mein**	"	*receive*

13. Write out at random ten words in the foreign language (at least five letters each). Then indicate the number of phonemes that make up each word.

Sample Answer:

French: travail (6), bonne (3), ancien (4), belle (3), vient (3), viennent (4), quatre (4), cinq (3), quatorze (6), vingt (2), commencer (6).

Spanish: (Note that in Spanish the number of orthographic symbols often corresponds to the number of phonemes): buscado (7), amo (3), querer (5), mucho (4), hombre (5), perro (4), pero (4), ella (3), amigos (6), huerta (5).

German: Biene (4), bitte (4), blau (4), blieb (4), Schiff (3), bleib (5), Schach (3), Knochen (6), Naht (3), Wiese (4).

12

Learning

Morphology

Some words are made up of just one morpheme (e.g., *house*, *fatigue*, *carry*), but many are made up of several morphemes. Remember that we distinguished root morphemes, derivational morphemes, and grammatical morphemes. You can use your knowledge of the root and derivational morphemes to figure out the meaning of words, but making up your own words on the analogy of others may get you into trouble. Yet as far as increasing your recognition or passive vocabulary is concerned, a knowledge of the meaning of the component building stones will increase your reading and comprehension ability quite considerably. Obviously you—or a foreigner learning English—do not have to have previous knowledge of a word like *generosity* if you are familiar with the adjective *generous* and know from other examples (e.g., *liberality*, *animosity*) that -*ity* is an ending that indicates a noun and carries the meaning "quality of." To give another example, once you know the meaning of the word *contest*, the word *incontestable* becomes quite clear, provided that you realize that *in-* carries the meaning of negation and that -*able* is a suffix used for adjectives. In English, just like most other languages, individual words—if they are made up of several building stones—need not be considered as separate items, the meaning of which must be learned individually. In most cases their meaning is simply the result of the meaning of their component parts.

When it comes to the morphemes that carry grammatical meaning, you must of course learn just how and when to use them actively in order to be able to speak the language. If you do not know how to use these grammatical endings you are either not able to talk at all, or you will make up forms and words that simply do not exist in the language. In our analysis of the possible errors in morphology, we have already stressed that the main danger involved—the main reason for making up "wrong" words—is simply the use of the wrong variant of a morpheme: *dishs* for *dishes*, *gived* for *gave*, etc. Note that actually there are two hurdles to overcome: you must know which morphemes to use, and you must be able to select the right variant. You must know both the *rule* and the *exception*.

The selection of the right morpheme and the right variant is ultimately a matter of practice and habit formation. The native speaker of English, and the foreigner who has learned to speak English fluently, will say *I gave him the dishes* quite automatically, without thinking of the fact that *gave* is an irregular past and that the plural of *dish* is *dishes* (not *dishs*) because the word ends in /ʃ/.

At the same time, however, conscious awareness of rule and exception—in other words, understanding of the dominant grammatical morpheme and its variants—will be of great help in the initial stages of learning. Generally the learner should realize that the exceptions are of two types: those that are by themselves clearly predictable (the ones that follow a rule within the rule), and those that are completely unpredictable. The most predictable exceptions are those in which the choice of a specific variant of a morpheme is dictated by the following or preceding sounds. The case of *dishes* is a good example. We have had others: the /t/ pronunciation of the past tense ending after unvoiced consonants (*laughed* /læft/) as opposed to the /d/ pronunciation after the voiced ones (*smiled* /smaɪld/); the /s/ pronunciation of the third person singular morpheme after voiceless consonants (*cuts* /kəts/); the /z/ pronunciation after vowels and voiced consonants (*studies* /stədiz/, *rubs* /rəbz/); the /ɪz/ pronunciation after sibilants (*wishes* /wɪʃɪz/). Such variations are learned best if the reason for the variation is clearly understood. Of course, as always, the understanding must be supplemented by practice.

When it comes to the unpredictable variations (e.g., *oxen* as plural of *ox*, *gave* as past of *give*) there is little that can be done *except to learn them*. What might prove helpful is a practice followed by many grammar books of *grouping* these exceptions and learning and practicing them in categories, rather than learning them as individual items. In other words, a student learning English might find it helpful to learn and practice the verbs *bet*, *burst*, *cast*, *cost*, *cut*, *hit*, etc. as a group (past and past participle formed by "zero allomorph"), *creep*, *deal*, *feel*, *keep*, *leap*, etc., as another group (past and past participle formed with *-t* and vowel change /i/ > /ε/), and so on.

In connection with learning how to form the words of a language, it is very important to realize that making up the word correctly or knowing how to recite forms in a "paradigmatic arrangement" is of little use unless you know how to use the forms. The most beautiful building block is useless if you don't know how to fit it into the larger pattern. It is essential therefore that learning words and word forms go hand in hand with learning how to fit these forms into the larger grammatical construction.

Put yourself in the situation of a learner of English who has memorized a paradigm, or a series of paradigms, like:

I	me	my	mine
you	you	your	yours
he	him	his	his
she	her	her	hers

Knowing the paradigms and the chart would, by itself, not necessarily keep you from producing sentences like: *He likes mine book* or *Me Tarzan*. At the same time the chart does contain a lot of valuable information and (especially if you are "visually minded") knowing the paradigms and remembering or visualizing the chart may turn out to be a great help. But in order to be able to utilize the chart fully, you would have to keep in mind a few facts: In learning the paradigm, you must realize that *I*, *me*, *my*, *mine* is a completely fortuitous or accidental arrangement; we could have written it *me*, *I*, *mine*, *my*. The sequence of the words in the paradigm means nothing. Usually it is determined by convention. Thus in languages in which the nouns have several cases, it is customary to put the nominative before the genitive, etc. In the preceding paradigm chart of the English pronoun, the important and valuable information is contained not in the horizontal arrangement, but in the *vertical column*. For the words that are in the same vertical column are substitutable for each other within the same sentence structure. The whole paradigm thus becomes meaningful if it is remembered in connection with sample sentences indicating the use of each vertical column: *I study at the university; MY brother gives me the book; This book is MINE.*

The principle we have just illustrated applies especially in languages in which the morphology is complicated—in which, for instance, the nouns have several cases (e.g., Latin, German, Russian). In any such language the memorization of paradigms and the remembering of paradigm charts (e.g., several noun declensions arranged systematically next to each other) can be of great help—*provided* that you visualize and associate the substitutable elements with each other and tie them in with specific sentence structures.

The principle just stated applies also to verbs, of course. Our foreign student may memorize:

speak	speaks	speaking	spoke	spoken
give	gives	giving	gave	given
sing	sings	singing	sang	sung

Yet learning the forms and knowing how to use them are two different tasks. The knowledge of the paradigm does not necessarily prevent errors like *I have spoke* or *I speaks*. Again the memorization of the paradigm and the visual memory of the paradigm chart must be supplemented by sample sentences, and by the realization that the elements arranged in vertical columns have identical grammatical functions. The paradigmatic chart can be tied in with the actual use of language in several ways. For example, let us assume that our foreign student studying English is strongly visually minded and has a good visual memory. He has learned and can recall the paradigm of the verb using the following chart:

	Present	Present Progressive	Past	Present Perfect
I	laugh	am laughing	laughed	have laughed
you	laugh	are laughing	laughed	have laughed
he	laughs	is laughing	laughed	has laughed

The chart contains all the grammatical morphemes used with English verbs. Once the student memorizes *give, gives, giving, gave, given*, he would know (on the anology of *laugh, laughs, laughing, laughed, laughed*) just where these irregular forms fit on the chart; but the important step would be to learn how to use the chart in order to form sentences.

Although our student may have already memorized *give, gives, gave, given* as a paradigm in that sequence, he may still have difficulty in thinking of the correct verb form quickly at the moment at which he must use it. Ultimately the use of the correct form must become a matter of instantaneous recall rather than the result of the recital of a paradigm. An empty chart like the following can be used rather

	Present	Present Progressive	Past	Present Perfect
I				
you				
he				

efficiently in training one to recall forms quickly without reference to a particular order. We could tell our foreign student to practice his English verb morphology in the following way: "Think of a sample sentence using the verb to be practiced, such as *I give him the book*. Then close your eyes, hit the empty verb chart with your pencil, open your eyes again, and see how quickly you can say the sentence with the form that corresponds to the empty slot in which your pencil happened to land." Thus if upon opening his eyes our student finds that the point of his pencil has come to rest in the first square of the fourth column, his answer or reflex should be *I have given him the book*. Ten minutes' practice daily (three or four irregular verbs for each session) would go a long way toward giving our student mastery of the morphology of the English verb pattern. Of course we should emphasize again that the ultimate aim of using a paradigmatic chart is to be able to get along without it. But at the same time, we should bear in mind that it affords systematization and use of visual memory, both of which may come in handy in the initial stages of instruction and learning, and especially with languages which (from the point of view of English at least) offer a bewildering variety of morphological endings.

Learning Exercises and Questions

1. Write out at least three words in a foreign language (each containing more than one morpheme). Then divide the words into morphemes and give one example of a word in which each morpheme is reused.

Sample Answer:

French: re/ten/ir: **re**/ven/ir; **ten**/ons; fin/**ir**
av/oir: **av**/ons; re/cev/**oir**
parl/ez: **parl**/ons; finiss/**ez**

Spanish: re/nov/ar: **re**/pet/ir; **nuev**/o; habl/**ar**
re/pel/ar: **re**/stitu/ir; **pel**/o; am/**ar**

(Note that you could actually subdivide the -ar ending of the infinitive into -a- and -r, -a- being the vowel indicating the type of conjugation, and only -r being the grammatical morpheme showing that the form is the infinitive.)

vis/ual/mente: **vis**/ión; man/**ual**; rar/a/**mente**

German: Rechn/ung: **rechn**/en; Wohn/**ung**
Nöt/ig/ung: **Not**; mut/*ig*; Mein/**ung**
zer/brech/en: **zer**/stören; er/**brech**/en; sag/**en**

2. Give at least four examples of morphemes that are characteristic for nouns and four that are characteristic for adjectives.

Sample Answer:

French: **-ité** (fraternité, égalité); **-eur** (professeur, docteur); **-ie** (académie, ironie); **-ion** (nation, illusion); **-eux, euse** (heureux, dangereux); **-if, -ive** (maladif, craintif); **-able** (coupable, désirable); **-al** (local, normal)

Spanish: **-or** (trabajador, hablador); **-ero** (torero, escudero); **-ía** (librería, panadería), **-ión** (nación, creación); **-oso** (hermoso, famoso); **-ario** (ordinario, vario); **-ivo** (intensivo, creativo); **-al** (natal, normal)

German: **-er** (Arbeiter, Schuster); **-e** (Höhe, Kälte); **-ling** (Jüngling, Liebling), **-heit** (Wahrheit, Einheit)

(Note that noun endings are normally associated with a specific gender.)

-ig (mutig, fleissig); **-lich** (königlich, kaiserlich); **-isch** (neidisch, Englisch); **-voll** (sorgenvoll, kummervoll)

3. Give at least one example of a "word family" that is formed by using various derivational morphemes with one root morpheme.

   Sample Answer:

   French: patin, patiner, patineur, patinage, etc.

   Spanish: libro, libreta, librito, librejo, libretín, libreto, libraco, librero, librote (*a bad book*), etc.

   German: Bund, Bündnis, Bündel, Ausbund, verbünden, etc.

4. Give some examples in a foreign language of "suppletion": the complete replacement of a root morpheme by another morpheme. (Example: *good, better.*)

   Sample Answer:

   French: The comparative (and superlative) of **bon** and **mauvais:** (le) meilleur, (le) pire. The comparative and superlative of **mal** and **bien:** (le) pis, (le) mieux. The verb **aller:** je vais, tu vas, il va, ils vont; j'irai, etc. The verb **être:** je suis, nous sommes, ils sont; je serai; je fus, etc.

   Spanish: The comparative (and superlative) of **bueno (bien)** and **malo (mal):** mejor, peor. The verb **ser:** fue, fuiste, etc. The verb **ir:** voy, vas, etc.

   German: The comparative and superlative of **gut:** besser, am besten. The verb **sein:** ich bin, ich war, etc.

5. Give at least one example of a variant of a morpheme, the use of which is determined by the "phonetic environment" (the preceding and/or following sounds).

Sample Answer:

French: This feature of morphemic alternation because of the following sound is one of the most characteristic of French. Think of all the orthographic final -*s*, -*t*, and -*n* symbols that become pronounced before a vowel. This is just another way of saying that words like **les, mes, nous, vous, mon,** etc., have one variant to be used before a consonant (**les livres,** pronounced /le livʀ/) and another variant before a vowel (les enfants, pronounced /lez ãfã/). Thus French will spell these morpheme variants the same, but the pronunciation is different.

Spanish: Some alternations in the morpheme are predictable on the basis of the rules of phonology alone: thus /n/ before *p*, *b* does not exist in Spanish and must be replaced by /m/: **un libro**/un libro/, but **un peso**/um peso/. Another morphemic alternation (not predictable on the basis of phonology, but dependent on the phonetic environment) is the use of the article **el** before feminine singular nouns beginning with a stressed *a*-: **el águila.** The plural morpheme of the nouns is normally -*s*, but -*es* after stems ending in consonants: **alumno, alumnos,** but **profesor, profesores.**

German: There is an alternation between -*s* and -*es* in the endings of the genitive of masculine nouns: **des Vaters, des Tisches.** -*s* rather than -*es* must be used if the preceding word has more than one syllable (unless the last syllable is stressed). **Graben, Vater, Vogel,** etc. can form the genitive only with -*s;* -*es* is utterly impossible.

6. Is the noun morphology of the foreign language you are studying complicated enough so that you could profit from a paradigmatic chart? If so, give an example of such a chart, and tell how to use it.

Answer:

French: No. French noun morphology is extremely simple. As a matter of fact, even the difference between singular and plural is normally signalled (in speech at least) by the word modifying the noun (e.g., the article) rather than by the noun itself. The final -*s* (or -*x*) that appears at the end of the noun is usually just an orthographic symbol. There are only a very few nouns in French in which the plural is signalled by the noun itself (e.g., **canal/canaux, oeil/yeux, oeuf/oeufs** (/ø/), **travail/travaux,** etc.).

Spanish: No. The only grammatical morpheme of the Spanish noun is the one indicating plural (-*s*, -*es*) and its rather rare variants.

German: Yes. A chart of the noun declension may help you to avoid confusion and to summarize your knowledge. Remember, however, that memorizing charts is by itself a fairly meaningless procedure. The advantage of the chart is to *systematize what you have learned*, and you must continuously tie in the chart with actual language. To give an example: The following is a conventional chart summarizing and giving examples of some of the major types in the masculine and feminine declensions.

		Masculine			Feminine	
S i n g .	Nom.	der Vater	der Mann	der Knabe	die Mutter	die Frau
	Gen.	des Vaters	des Mannes	des Knaben	der Mutter	der Frau
	Dat.	dem Vater	dem Mann(e)	dem Knaben	der Mutter	der Frau
	Acc.	den Vater	den Mann	den Knaben	die Mutter	die Frau
P l .	Nom.	die Väter	die Männer	die Knaben	die Mütter	die Frauen
	Gen.	der Väter	der Männer	der Knaben	der Mütter	der Frauen
	Dat.	den Vätern	den Männern	den Knaben	den Müttern	den Frauen
	Acc.	die Väter	die Männer	die Knaben	die Mütter	die Frauen

Remember now that in this chart the vertical sequence is fortuitous, but that the words in the same horizontal row are substitutable for each other. Now make up "sentence frames" for each of the four cases:

1. _____(Nom.)_____ ist (sind) hier.
2. Ich suche das Buch _____(Gen.)_____ .
3. Das Buch gehört _____(Dat.)_____ .
4. Ich sehe _____(Acc.)_____ .

Use the words on the chart in these sentence frames: **Der Vater ist hier. Der Mann ist hier. Ich suche das Buch des Vaters. Ich suche das Buch des Mannes. Das Buch gehört dem Knaben. Das Buch gehört der Mutter. Ich sehe die Mutter. Ich sehe die Frau,** etc.

Next step: take other words that you want to practice and put them into the same sentences (e.g., **der Schüler, der Lehrer, der Riese, die Tochter, die Lehrerin,** etc.). If you have any difficulty or are not sure of your answer, refer back to the chart.

Finally, make yourself a blank chart:

Singular
Nom.
Gen.
Dat.
Acc.
Plural
Nom.
Gen.
Dat.
Acc.

Now think of the noun that you want to practice (e.g., **der Lehrer**). Close your eyes and touch your chart with a pencil. If your pencil comes down on Dative Singular, say the sentence that requires the use of the dative (e.g., **Das Buch gehört dem Lehrer**). (If you have any trouble or are not sure of your answer, check again with the original chart.) In this kind of practice, the paradigm chart will help you to learn the grammatical forms and to tie them in with actual constructions.

7. Is the verb morphology complicated enough so that you could use a paradigm chart? If so, how could it be used?

Answer: A verb chart could certainly be used effectively in French, Spanish, and German as well as in many other languages. Remember again that it is not a question of memorizing a chart, but of using it for the purpose of systematizing and practicing what you have learned. Make yourself a grid with the personal subject pronouns on the left and the names of the tenses at the top:

	Present	Imperfect	Future	etc.
je (yo, ich)				
tu (tú, du)				
il (él, er)				
nous (nosotros, wir)				
vous (vosotros, ihr)				
ils (ellos, sie)				

Include all the important tenses. If you are still learning the language, add the new tenses as you learn them. Then practice verbs (especially irregular ones) by putting them into a sample sentence (normally in the first person singular present). Close your eyes, touch your practice grid with your pencil, and repeat the sentence with the verb in the exact form that fills the square in which your pencil is resting. *Make sure that you know the exact meaning of the sentence you have produced.* If you cannot produce the correct form, look it up (most grammar books have lists of the irregular verbs and conjugational charts). See whether you can work up speed in producing the correct answers.

13

Learning Words
and Their Meaning

The problem connected with learning words of a foreign language
—aside from the obvious task of memorizing them—is invariably the
possibility of some sort of confusion. This confusion can be caused
either by the sound or symbol part of the word or by its meaning.
Confusions caused by the sound or symbol part can be of two
kinds, both equally dangerous, both to be avoided. The symbols
(spoken or written) that express a particular meaning may be so
similar to those used to express a different meaning that the learner
has difficulty in keeping them apart. In this particular case the
symbols or arrangement of symbols that could be confused must be
contrasted with each other, so that the learner becomes aware of the
difference. For example, as a native speaker of English you will not
get confused in the usage and the meanings of *get up, get out, get along,
get over, get away,* etc., or *take up, take over, take on,* etc. However, to a
foreigner learning English, the multiplicity of meanings that can be
expressed by simply varying the word with which *take, get, make,* etc.
can be combined represents a baffling problem. He has no trouble
distinguishing the concept of *get up* from that of *get off,* but he will
wonder which means which; was it *get off* that means this thing you
do after you awake in the morning?—and when I do not know at

which stop of the streetcar the university is located, should I ask the driver where to *get up* or *get off?* Many of these combinations (e.g., *take up, take over*) are in fact two-part verbs (which we discussed in Chapter 4), while other combinations of verb + preposition or verb + adverb are simply idiomatic expressions, i.e., their meaning is not predictable from their component parts (e.g., *get along, get away*).

The other possibility of a confusion caused by the symbols themselves comes from the native language. Here you must be continuously on the lookout for words that sound nearly (and sometimes almost exactly) like a word of your own language, but that mean something entirely different. The particular danger is of course that the misuse of the foreign word may lead not only to a misunderstanding, but even to a complete breakdown of communication. There is a big difference between getting a book in the library or in the bookstore, just as there is between assisting at an operation or just watching it. But these are just two examples of the trouble that the so-called "false cognates" can create. The only real protection against the false cognates is learning them. This means you must simply remember that **librería** (**librairie**) means *bookstore* in Spanish (or French) and not *library*, and at the same time learn that a *library* is **biblioteca** (**bibliothèque**) in those languages. Fortunately, most textbooks point out the most dangerous of the false cognates, and many contain special exercises dealing with them.

Most problems in vocabulary confusion, however, are not created by the pupil's getting confused by the symbols. The confusion usually involves the meaning itself. There are many reasons for this type of confusion. Often the native language will not make a distinction between two concepts, while the foreign language will. Many foreigners learning English will say *I'll walk with you until the door* or *I stay with you as far as six o'clock.* Their language does not distinguish between the time and space dimensions when expressing the idea of *up to a certain point.* To the speaker of English the distinction between a familiar *you* and a polite *you* may be very puzzling. Why should Spanish need two words for *to be?* And why two words in French, Spanish, and German for *to know?* And the speaker of French or Spanish may wonder why English needs *do* and *make;* they both express the same concept as far as he is concerned. Why subdivide it? The only solution, as far as the learner is concerned, is to be watchful, to try to recognize from whatever cues he might get just how and why the foreign language introduces distinctions where his language does not. But the main advice that one can give the foreign language learner is the following:

1. Words "mean" something only in a specific situation. The only meaning of a foreign word that you can really know and be sure of is the one associated with the particular situation in which you have met it in the first place. Situation, here, means the construction in which the word is used as well as the meaning associated with it.
2. The only time you can really be sure that you are using a foreign word correctly is if you use it in a situation that is identical or nearly identical to the one in which you learned it in the first place.
3. The more dissimilar the situation in which you are using the word is from the one in which it was first learned, the more likely is the chance of error.
4. From the above considerations, it follows that any word should preferably be learned in the context of a situation and of a grammatical construction. Without such a context, you have no way of judging the appropriateness of its use.
5. Remembering the simple equivalent of the foreign words in the native language is therefore a very poor way of learning the meaning of a word, because it provides for no context whatsoever. Remembering simple equivalents is a fairly safe way of learning words only if the meanings involved are very obvious, concrete and definite concepts: e.g., objects like *hat, hand, glove, table;* animals like *cat, horse,* etc.; but even there you might run into trouble. For example, Spanish does not always use the same words for corresponding parts of the body of animals and humans, German uses a word for *eating* when done by animals that is derogatory if applied to the same activity by humans.

As a matter of fact, as we have stressed already, most errors in vocabulary are due to the fact that a foreign word has been equated with a word of the native language. This equation has been brought about either because the learner has consciously memorized it (e.g., French **faire** = *do* or *make*) or because he has associated the words through a specific utterance (*I do my homework* = **Je fais mon devoir**). When the occasion arises, the learner extends the possible usage of the "equivalent" of his own language (e.g., **Je fais des souliers** = *I do shoes*) and is likely to make a mistake. Sometimes the mistakes are almost unavoidable, but even the beginner can cut down on their number if he keeps in mind our suggestion to be cautious about extending the usage of a word according to the pattern of his native language.

Before extending the use of a word according to one's native pattern, one should quickly consider two questions: (1) Is the foreign word going to be used in the same type of construction in which he met it before? (2) Does it really mean the same thing? To give examples, you learn in language X the expression for *Charles is making automobiles*, and with it a foreign equivalent for *make*. Then you want to express the idea *Charles is making his wife very happy*. The mere fact that *make* will now have to be used in a completely different construction (with an adjective rather than a noun) should make you hesitate before using the same word you used earlier. You are, so to speak, proceeding at your own risk. (Incidentally, you *could* use the same word in German, but not in French or Spanish.) When it comes to extending the meaning from the original situation, you must make a comparison between the meaning of the word in that situation and the one in which you want to use it. Languages have a way of extending the meaning of words from a very concrete original meaning to more abstract meanings and "idiomatic" or special usages in which the original meaning is in fact no longer recognizable, or is used in a figurative way. If you know a foreign word equivalent in any one of these meaning situations, keep in mind that most likely the equivalence will break down in the other situations. Many vocabulary mistakes are made because the learner assumes rather naively that the foreign language will follow the pattern of his own in transferring a word from the concrete to the abstract or in using it figuratively. Just because you may know the foreign language equivalent of *I got a package* (and with it an equivalent of *got*), you have no right to assume that this equivalent can be transferred into the situation of *I got excited* (note the change in construction), of *I got the idea* (figurative meaning = *I understood the idea*). Or knowing the equivalent of *fire* as a result of learning the expression for *fire a rocket* is not likely to equip you with the right expression for *Firing Mr. Jones for inefficiency*.

Learning Exercises and Questions

1. Write out three idiomatic expressions of English. Remember that idiomatic expressions are those which have a meaning that cannot be deduced from the component elements.

Sample Answer: 1. He has nothing on me. 2. John and Mary made up after their quarrel. 3. He always has the upper hand.

2. (a) Write at least four sentences in which the word *get* is used with different meanings. (b) Write out six sentences in which the word *get* is used with different adverbs.

Sample Answer: (a) 1. I got a letter. 2. I got excited. 3. He got to work late. 4. I finally got (understood) his explanation. (b) 1. I get up at six. 2. He got away. 3. He's getting along fine. 4. He's getting over his cold. 5. This is getting me down. 6. Where do I get off?

3. Give three examples of the usage of a word in a concrete and then in an abstract or figurative sense.

Sample Answer: 1. He picked up the book. Where did you pick up your French? 2. She gathered some flowers. I gather that you do not agree. 3. The cat rubbed against my leg. His suggestion rubbed me the wrong way.

4. The following is an exercise in developing sensitivity to the possibility of transferring words from one situation to another. You are given a sentence in which one word is *italicized*. The same italicized word then appears in three other sentences (a), (b), and (c). You are to select the sentence in which the use of the italicized word is most like that in the original sentence, i.e., is most likely to have the same foreign language vocabulary equivalent as in the original sentence.

Example: Charles is *leaving* Paris.

    (a) Charles is *leaving* Germany.
    (b) Charles stays here but Robert is *leaving*.
    (c) I shall *leave* the decision to you.

Your answer should be (a). (b) uses a different construction (no direct object), and (c) uses the word in a meaning radically different from that of the original sentence.

Part A

1. He was a very *able* man.

   (a) I am not *able* to follow him.
   (b) Charles is not as *able* as his brother.
   (c) All *able*-bodied men will be drafted.

2. I do not want to talk *about* him.

   (a) They came at *about* six o'clock.
   (b) We had a disagreement *about* this matter.
   (c) The children were playing *about* in the garden.

3. You try to help people, but all you get is *abuse*.

   (a) Naturally with *abuse* the engine will break down.
   (b) I do not have to take this sort of *abuse* from you.
   (c) This is an *abuse* of presidential power.

4. Charles found the solution by *accident*.

   (a) Robert had an *accident* in his car.
   (b) Our father's *accident* caused us a great deal of concern.
   (c) We cannot leave the outcome of this struggle to chance and *accident*.

5. His pain was quite *acute*.

   (a) The danger has indeed become *acute*.
   (b) That is a very *acute* observation.
   (c) His hearing is not as *acute* as mine.

6. He asked for an *advance* in salary from seventy to eighty dollars weekly.

   (a) There has been a steady *advance* in prices.
   (b) John got an *advance* in rank. He is now a major.
   (c) Jack asked for an *advance* on his next month's allowance in order to buy football tickets.

7. Robert and I are the same *age*.

   (a) During the *age* of the Pharaohs Egypt was a powerful country.

(b) Robert will come of *age* on his next birthday.

(c) At your *age* you should be more careful.

8. Charles *became* our leader.

(a) The situation has *become* quite complicated.

(b) It does not *become* you to talk like that to your parents.

(c) This dress does not *become* you at all.

9. Do you *know* this man?

(a) I *know* that you are wrong.

(b) I don't *know* just what to tell you.

(c) Unfortunately, I do not *know* this country.

10. Don't *apply* a bandage to this wound.

(a) The decision does not *apply* in this case.

(b) You should *apply* glue if you want to mend the chair.

(c) Charles didn't even *apply* for the job.

Answers (to Part A): 1. (b) 2. (b) 3. (b) 4. (c) 5. (c) 6. (c) 7. (c) 8. (a) 9. (c) 10. (b) (The possible translations were compared with German.)

Part B

1. Why don't you *close* the window?

(a) Please *close* your eyes.

(b) The session will *close* at nine.

(c) We must *close* ranks behind our leader.

2. I would like to *meet* Mr. Smith.

(a) When shall we three *meet* again?

(b) I hope this suggestion *meets* with your approval.

(c) I am very happy to *meet* you.

3. This situation *looks* quite promising.

(a) Please *look* before crossing the street.

(b) I like this dress. How does it *look* on me?

(c) Charles certainly *looks* good these days.

4. Robert *lives* on the third floor.

(a) Grandfather *lived* for eighty years.
(b) Charles has never *lived* in England.
(c) They *lived* happily ever after.

5. Charles *left* Paris ten years ago.

(a) Charlotte decided to *leave* her husband.
(b) The train *left* the station at five.
(c) Will you please *leave* me alone!

6. May I *keep* this as a souvenir?

(a) Can you *keep* a secret?
(b) I wonder what kind of company he *keeps*.
(c) Charles never *keeps* a promise.

7. Charles certainly was *mad* when he received your letter.

(a) His plan to overthrow the government was completely *mad*.
(b) When I told him the truth he got *mad* at me.
(c) I am glad the dog that bit you was not *mad*.

8. John certainly has a brilliant *mind*.

(a) Unfortunately Charles has again changed his *mind*.
(b) I wish you would speak your *mind*.
(c) At the age of eighty, his *mind* is not what it used to be.

9. Although the animal was dead, its body still *moved*.

(a) Robert seemed *moved* by your story.
(b) There were so many people in the room it was difficult to *move*.
(c) Roger has just *moved* to Paris.

10. At this point it is possible to look across the *narrow* straits.

(a) We had a very *narrow* escape.
(b) This is a very *narrow* interpretation of your responsibilities.
(c) We had difficulty getting through the *narrow* door.

Answers (to Part B): 1. (a) 2. (c) 3. (c) 4. (b) 5. (b)
6. (a) 7. (b) 8. (c) 9. (b) 10. (c) (The possible translations were compared with French.)

Answer exercises 5 through 9 with reference to any foreign language
you know or are studying. Sample answers are provided for French,
Spanish, and German.

5. Does the foreign language contain many words or expressions
   that are likely to be confusing because of similarity with each
   other in sound or writing? Give some examples.

   Sample Answer:

   French: An example might be **part, parti, partie: Il ne
   faisait pas partie de mes amis** [*He was not part of (among)
   my friends*]; **Il m'a fait part de ses intentions** (*He informed
   me of his intentions*); **Il est membre du parti conservateur**
   (*He is a member of the Conservative party*).

   Other examples: **jeune** (*young*), **jeûne** (*fasting*); **baiser**
   (*kiss*), **baisser** (*to lower*). The similarity of construction may
   create confusion between **J'ai manqué le train** (*I missed the
   train*) and **Mes parents me manquent** (*I miss my parents*).

   Spanish: A few examples are **sentir** (*to feel*), **sentar** (*to sit*);
   partido (*political party, match*); **partida** (*departure*); **puñado**
   (*fistful*), **puñada** (*a blow*); **el capital** (*the capital; money*),
   la capital (*the capital; city*).

   German: The possibility of mix-ups within the language is a
   fairly important and serious category of error in German.
   There are, for instance, many verbs (often historically related) that are differentiated only by one sound, and that
   have quite different meanings (although they may be in
   related areas of meaning). To give a few examples: **liegen/
   legen; bitten/bieten/beten; fahren/führen; rennen/
   rinnen; kennen/können; wiegen/wagen; stehlen/stel-
   len; reisen/reissen; mahlen/malen** (phonetically identical). If you are confused by the similarity of verbs such as
   these, be sure to learn and remember them in contrasting

sentences: e.g., **Das Buch liegt auf dem Tisch. Ich lege das Buch auf den Tisch. Ich bete zu Gott. Ich bitte um ein Stück Brot. Ich biete hundert Mark für dieses Buch.** Even more confusing than the pairs of similar verbs are perhaps the German "two-part verbs." As a rule these are separable if the stress, in the infinitive, is on the preposition: e.g., infinitive **wiéderholen** (*get again*): **Haben Sie das Buch wieder geholt?** Infinitive **wiederhólen** (*repeat, review*): **Haben Sie das Buch wiederhólt?** Since in the infinitive the only difference between the forms (which mean very different things) is in the stress, confusion is likely to occur. Again, similar verbs must be learned in contrasting examples. Another area of possible confusion within German are nouns that are differentiated only by their gender: **der Gehalt** (*the contents*), **das Gehalt** (*the salary*); **der Band** (*the volume*), **das Band** (*the ribbon*); **der Leiter** (*the leader*), **die Leiter** (*the ladder*); etc.

6. Can you give the example of four words in which the similarity with English may be a cause of error? Give an example of their correct use and an example of the words that the foreign language would have to use to express the meaning of the English word that caused the confusion.

Sample Answer:

French:

1. **monnaie**/*money*
   Gardez la **monnaie** (Keep the *change*); J'ai assez d'**argent** (I have enough *money*).

2. **figure**/*figure*
   Jeanne s'est lavé la **figure** (Jean washed her *face*); Elle a une belle **silhouette** (She has a good *figure*).

3. **déception**/*deception*
   Vous pouvez imaginer quelle était ma **déception** (You can imagine my *disappointment*); Vous ne pouvez pas réussir par cette sorte de **fraude** (You can't succeed with this sort of *deception*).

4. **lecture**/*lecture*
J'ai fini la **lecture** de ce livre (I finished *reading* this book); J'ai assisté à sa **conférence** (I attended his *lecture*).

Spanish:

1. **actual**/*actual*
Sus intereses **actuales** no son los mismos (His *present* interests are not the same); El **verdadero** jefe del gobierno es el presidente (The *actual* head of the government is the president.)

2. **librería**/*library*
Compré el libro en la **librería** (I bought the book in the *bookstore*); No pude hallar el libro en la **biblioteca** (I couldn't find the book in the *library*).

3. **particular**/*particular*
A Juan le hacen falta lecciones **particulares** de francés (John needs *private* lessons in French); No conozco los **detalles** (I am not familiar with the *particulars*); Me acuerdo de **cierta** contestación (I remember a particular *answer*).

4. **colorado**/*colored*
La tierra del país es **colorada** (The earth in this area is *reddish*); Yo vi a un hombre **de color** (I saw a *colored* man).

German:

1. **bekommen**/*become*
Karl hat einen Brief **bekommen** (Charles *received* a letter); Karl wurde sehr **aufgeregt** (Charles *became* very excited).

2. **Lust**/*lust*
Ich habe **Lust** ins Kino zu gehen (I *feel like* going to the movies); Man muss **Wollust** von Liebe unterscheiden (One must distinguish *lust* from love).

3. **brav**/*brave*
Die Kinder sind heute sehr **brav** (The children are very *well behaved* today); Die Soldaten sind **tapfer** (The soldiers are *brave*).

4. **blamieren**/*blame*
   Karl hat sich wirklich **blamiert** (Charles really *made* a fool of himself); Ich werde meine Freunde nicht **beschuldigen** (I won't *blame* my friends).

7. Give at least three instances in which the foreign language makes a compulsory distinction within a concept by using different words, while English covers the same ground with just one expression. Illustrate your examples.
   Sample Answer:

French:

1. English *day*/French **jour, journée**
   Ma premiere **journée** à Paris était très interéssante. J'ai passé trous **jours** à Paris.

2. English *in* (with time expressions)/French **dans, en**
   Je ferais ça **dans** une heure (*within* the next hour). Je peux faire ça **en** une heure (it will take me one hour).

3. English *know*/French **connaître, savoir**
   Je **connais** M. Smith. Je **sais** que vous avez raison.

Spanish:

1. English *to be*/Spanish **ser, estar, hacer, tener, hay,** etc.
   Jorge **es** inteligente. Jorge **está** cansado. **Hace** frio. **Tengo** miedo. **Hay** muchos alumnos en esta clase.

2. English *know*/Spanish **saber, conocer**
   Sé que Ud. tiene razón. **Conozco** al señor Smith.

3. English *before*/Spanish **antes de** (time), **delante de** (place)
   Salí **antes de** las ocho. El alumno está **delante de** mí.

German:

1. English *know*/German **wissen, kennen**
   Ich **weiss** die Antwort nicht. Ich **kenne** Herrn Schmidt

2. English *where*/German **wo, wohin**
   Wohin gehen Sie heute abend? **Wo** ist der Bahnhof?

3. English *you*/German **Sie, du**
   Was machst **du** denn, Karl? Was studieren **Sie**, Herr Professor?

8. Can you think of examples in which the foreign language must use two or more different *grammatical* categories (e.g., tenses) to express ideas that English can express with the same category. This means that the word which "corresponds" to the English word is the same but must be used in different forms.

Sample Answer:

French: The best example is the English use of the past tense as opposed to the French past indefinite (passé composé) and imperfect (l'imparfait). English uses the past for a simple completed action: *Yesterday I went to the movies;* for a repeated or habitual action in the past: *Last year I went to the movies every Saturday;* and sometimes for an action that was in progress or for a description: *Yesterday I worked in the garden while my brother stayed at home; The weather was beautiful.* French would use the past indefinite for the completed action: **Hier je suis allé au cinéma;** and the imperfect for the repeated action, the description, and the action in progress: **L'année passée j'allais au cinéma chaque samedi; Je travaillais dans le jardin pendant que mon frère restait à la maison; Il faisait beau temps.**

Spanish: English may use the past tense where Spanish must distinguish between the preterite and the imperfect. The preterite is the completed past action: **Ayer vi a mi amigo** (*Yesterday I saw my friend*). The imperfect is used for the action in progress, the recurrent action, or description of a condition: **Trabajaba mientras que Carlos me miraba** (*I worked while Charles watched*); **El año pasado iba allá todos los días** (*Last year I went there every day*); **El agua estaba fría** (*The water was cold*).

German: In German the use of the subjunctive versus an indicative can express nuances of meaning that English could not express—at least not by a change in the form of the verb. **Ich habe gelesen, dass er sehr gut Deutsch spricht.**

Ich habe gelesen dass er sehr gut Deutsch spräche. (In both cases, *I have read that he speaks German very well*.) The choice of the subjunctive **spräche** implies that the speaker has doubts about the truth of what he has read.

9. Many English words can be used in two or more different situations requiring the use of different foreign words to convey their meanings. Give five pairs of English sentences, each pair illustrating one such word, and the equivalent foreign sentences.

Sample Answer:

French:

1. I am *leaving* you this book.   Je vous **laisse** ce livre.
   I am *leaving* for Paris.   Je **pars** pour Paris.

2. Charles *is* cold.   Charles **a** froid.
   Charles *is* intelligent.   Charles **est** intelligent.

3. Marie is *making* progress.   Marie **fait** des progrés.
   Marie is *making* me happy.   Marie me **rend** heureux.

4. *Keep* your promise.   **Tenez** votre promesse.
   Keep your money.   **Gardez** votre argent.

5. What *time* is it?   Quelle **heure** est-il?
   I haven't any *time* to do this.   Je n'ai pas le **temps** de faire cela.

Spanish:

1. I have two *children*.   Tengo dos **hijos**.
   These *children* are beautiful.   Estos **niños** son hermosos.

2. Charles *runs* very fast.   Carlos **corre** muy rápidamente.

   My watch doesn't *run*.   Mi reloj no **anda**.

3. I'll *ask* for information.   **Pediré** informaciones.
   I'll *ask* a question.   **Haré** una pregunta.

4. I *am* intelligent.   **Soy** inteligente.
   I *am* hungry.   **Tengo** hambre.

5. What *time* is it?   ¿Que **hora** es?
   He did this for the first *time*.   Hizo esto por la primera **vez.**

German:

1. I *know* Mr. Jones.   Ich **kenne** Herrn Jones.
   I don't *know* the answer.   Ich **weiss** die Antwort nicht.

2. I *work* too much.   Ich **arbeite** zu viel.
   This machine doesn't *work*.   Diese Maschine **funktioniert** nicht.

3. *Last* year I went to Paris.   **Letztes** Jahr bin ich nach Paris gegangen.

   Last night I went to the movies.   **Gestern** abend bin ich ins Kino gegangen.

4. This exam was very *hard*.   Diese Prüfung war sehr **schwer.**

   His heart is as *hard* as stone.   Sein Herz ist **hart** wie Stein.

5. What *time* is it?   Wieviel **Uhr** ist es?
   I don't have *time* for this.   Dafür habe ich keine **Zeit.**

14

Learning

Syntactical

Patterns

In our discussion of learning vocabulary we did not include consideration of the function words. As we have stressed before, these words are part of the syntactical pattern and function only partly in conveying *word meaning*. Their main function is to convey *grammatical meaning*, in other words to show how the units of the sentence are related or to which word classes the words belong. What in English is represented by function words is in many languages represented by grammatical endings. English itself has at least one grammatical ending that can be equated with a function word, namely the *s* of the possessive function of the noun: My father's garden = the garden of my father.

One good way of demonstrating the operation of function words and the grammatical meanings they convey is to apply grammatical structure to nonsense syllables. We stated earlier that these nonsense syllables suddenly become "words" simply because we treat them as such from the grammatical point of view. A favorite example among linguists for the demonstration of grammatical function in isolation is Lewis Carroll's poem "Jabberwocky" in *Through the Looking Glass*:

(A)   (B) (C)

'Twas *brillig* and the *slithy toves*

<pre>
        (D)   (E)   (F)
    Did *gyre* and *gimble* in the *wabe;*
        (G)   (H)
    All *mimsy* were the *borogoves,*
        (I) (J)   (K)
    And the *mome raths outgrabe.*
</pre>

The italicized words of the poem are "non-sense" words. They are held together by function words and grammatical patterning. The nonsense words tell a story—a story told by grammatical meaning alone without the help of lexical meaning. If we look at the nonsense words, one after the other, we see that the spot of (A) could be filled by either a noun or an adjective (*'Twas summer,* *'Twas peaceful,* etc.). However (C) is unambiguously a noun because of the preceding *the* and the *did* that follows. (B), because of its position before the noun and its ending (*y*), is clearly marked as an adjective. (D) and (E) are felt as verbs because of the preceding *did.* (F), preceded by the unambiguous noun marker *the,* must be a noun. In the third line the plural function verb *were* and the plural marker *s* at the end of (H) indicate that this word, preceded by *the,* must be a plural noun and subject of the sentence; (G), not marked as a plural and ending in a derivational morpheme used for adjectives, is immediately classified as such. In the last line you probably interpreted (J) as a plural noun, subject of the sentence. Because of the English rule of position of adjectives, this would immediately make (I) an adjective and (K) a verb [probably an irregular verb in the past—the rest of the "story" is in the past, cf. *were* (line 3), *was* (line 1), and *outgrabe* sounds like the past of a verb *outgribe; give/gave, outgribe/outgrabe*—why not?]. Note, however, that the last line could be interpreted differently: e.g., if (I) is a noun, then (J) could also be a noun, but the object of the verb (K). This possibility is somewhat farfetched, but in a poem it is conceivable to have that kind of word order: *The mome raths outgrabe—the ruler peace proclaimed* (instead of the *ruler proclaimed peace*). Of course if our English vocabulary only included either the word *mome* or *raths,* the ambiguity would be resolved.

Poems like Carroll's "Jabberwocky" underline the tremendous importance of being able to recognize structural signals and grammatical patterns. Your ability to comprehend the spoken or written form of *any* language (including your own) depends largely on the quick "deciphering" of the signals that carry the structural meaning. In your native language you have the ability to comprehend these signals instantly in their spoken form. When it comes to reading, you should have the ability to understand the written counterparts of those structural signals almost as rapidly as if they had come to you through speech. A person who does not will probably be a slow reader and have difficulty assimilating materials rapidly.

We have shown in the analysis of "Jabberwocky" how the recognition of the structural signal goes a long way in helping us to make sense out of what would otherwise be just a complete garble of nonsense syllables. This same process is characteristic of the comprehension of real language just as it is of the "comprehension" of nonsense words. Once you have acquired a knowledge of structure and a limited vocabulary, you can use this knowledge to help you to understand new words and to comprehend sentences that are—partially at least—made up of unknown words. As a matter of fact, this process of starting with a limited vocabulary and a knowledge of grammatical structure and using these initial assets for increasing your ability in the language is precisely the same process that you have used (and should use) in your native language. You increase your English vocabulary and your sensitivity to English structure and usage by a great deal of reading. Note also that in this process you will usually not go to the dictionary to look up the meaning of words. This looking up—while necessary and advisable in some cases—could be overdone and slow up your reading to the point where it would most certainly become unenjoyable. In fact you learn most words simply by meeting and becoming acquainted with them. Most of the time you don't remember how you learned new words and you are not even conscious of learning them. You absorb their meaning because of two important helps at your disposal: (1) a general knowledge of the context, the situation in which the words are used, and (2) the knowledge of the grammatical structure in which the words are used. This grammatical structure not only supplies part of the meaning, it also helps to define the words grammatically.

Even if your goal in foreign language learning is to acquire a reading knowledge, it is thus very important that you learn to understand the structural signals quickly and easily. In most situations

(1) a knowledge of structure, (2) knowledge of "vocabulary" (i.e., knowledge of the words carrying lexical meaning), and (3) knowledge of the general context or situation in which language is used will combine and interact to convey the meaning of what is being expressed. Sometimes knowledge in one or two of these areas can be used to make up for lack of knowledge in the others. Thus people who know the technical vocabulary of their field of specialization (e.g., mathematics, chemistry, economics) in a foreign language are sometimes able to read technical materials in the foreign language even if their knowledge of the grammar is very poor. In a sense they are doing the exact reverse of what you as a native speaker of English could do with "Jabberwocky": they know the meaning of the words that have lexical significance and use the lexical meaning to supply the grammatical meaning (which for them, since they do not know the grammar, is made up of nonsense words and syllables like *the*, *will*, *-s*, *-y*, *may*, etc., and perhaps a strange and therefore meaningless word order). The writer of this book has heard of at least one case where knowledge of the general context or situation was used to make up for all the factors that normally interact to supply meaning. The experiment that the Russian scientist Pavlov performed with his dog is very well known and is described in most elementary textbooks of psychology. A graduate student, who had little or no knowledge of French was asked to give an English summary of a French text for his reading examination in French. In the French text he recognized the name Pavlov, and the word *chien* (dog). He passed the examination. Yet the instances in which you can rely on context, situation, and knowledge of vocabulary to make up for the lack of an understanding of structure will normally be few and limited. Situations are unpredictable and the vocabulary of a language is vast. Only structure and grammar are limited and finite. In other words, in most instances in which you want to understand the foreign language you will not be able to get along without the help that comes from structure and grammar, and—just as in your native language—you will most likely have to use it to fill the *lacunae* that exist in your knowledge of the vocabulary items. (Did you grasp the meaning of the italicized word from the context?)

When it comes to speaking the language, the necessity for the control of structure is obvious. We have already stressed the idea that probably the best way of speaking a foreign language is to remember sentences in the language and to convert them into what you want to say. In order to go through this conversion process, you must have some idea of the structure or grammar of the foreign language. This does not mean that you must necessarily be able to analyze a sentence and identify parts of speech, but it does mean that you must know what part of a sentence that you have learned is basic to the structure and what is a replaceable vocabulary item.

Assume for a moment that you are teaching English to a foreign student who, because of interference coming from his native language, says sentences like: *I have Charles recently seen, I have him the book given*, etc. Wouldn't it be a good idea to have him *say* and *remember* many sentences like *I have seen Charles recently, I have given him the book*, and at the same time get across the idea that he can use these sentences as models to form many others of the same grammatical construction? For the purpose of giving this kind of practice and creating the realization of "model" and "pattern," we use the so-called substitution exercises that are found in many grammars. The pupil is given a sentence, e.g., *I have not given him the money*, and the teacher shows, first by example, how this sentence can be changed by varying the words carrying lexical meaning without changing the grammatical construction:

I have not given him the money.   The teacher then says:

you	and models the answer	*You have not given him the money.*
sent	"	*You have not sent him the money.*
her	"	*You have not sent her the money.*
letter	"	*You have not sent her the letter.*

Once the pupil has observed and repeated after the teacher, he will provide the answer himself if he gets the substitution word as a cue. For example, let us assume that you are learning English as a foreign language. Your base sentence is *We did not understand this idea.*

The teacher says *you;* you respond:	*You did not understand this idea.*
" " *study;* " "	*You did not study this idea.*
" " *problem;* " "	*You did not study this problem.*

and so on.

This procedure would not only give you practice in saying these sentences, but more importantly, the next time you had to say *We*

did not understand this book, or *We did not find the book*, you would probably remember the sentence that you had practiced and convert it
into the sentence that you wanted to say, by the very substitution
procedure that was part of your practice session. It is for this reason
that it is very important that you do not go through the substitution
procedure mechanically, but try to associate each sentence with a
situation in which it could possibly be used. If you don't do this,
the sentences will probably not suggest themselves again as possible
responses or as models for possible responses.

Let us assume once more that we are teaching English to a foreign
student who can very accurately say sentences like: *I speak English
and I understand you very well*. But when it comes to the negative, he
says *I not speak English, I not understand you*. We can at least interpret
his difficulty as due to the fact that he does not know how to make
positive sentences negative, most likely because his native language
does it differently. So we want to give this student practice in the
correct way to make positive sentences negative. Not only will this
kind of practice force him to say a lot of correct negative sentences,
but it will also show him how to make up negative sentences if and
when he must do so on his own. So we have our student practice an
exercise that consists of transforming sentences like *I speak English* to
I don't speak English. After this procedure has been modeled by the
teacher, the positive sentences serve merely as cues. Putting yourself now into the student's situation, what will be your response if
the teacher says:

I follow your advice. You will say: *I don't follow your advice.*
I write poetry.   "   "   "   *I don't write poetry.*
I love Joan.   "   "   "   *I don't love Joan.*

and so on.

The procedure and goal of foreign language learning is then
simply the following: *to have at your disposal an ever-growing stock of
model sentences associated with specific situations that you can transform into
what you want to say by a limited number of substitution and transformation
procedures that you learn to perform at ever-increasing speed.*

Just what are the substitution and transformation procedures involved? Of course they will vary according to the foreign language
involved, but we can give a general classification from the point of
view of English—a classification that will be applicable to most of

the languages you are likely to study. This means that the categories that we mention will be usable, although the operations involved will take various and different forms.

The ways of creating new sentences out of old ones involve first of all a series of operations which we might classify as:

A. REPLACEMENT PROCEDURES

When you use a replacement operation, you do not change the basic structure of the model sentence, but simply replace one element by another identical element. The most important replacement procedures are:

(1) *Noun replacement:* Simply substitute one noun for another:

The *child* came late. ⟶ The *boy* came late.
I saw the *man.* ⟶ I saw the *dog.*

(2) *Pronoun replacement:* Replace a noun by a pronoun or a pronoun by another pronoun:

I saw *the man.* ⟶ I saw *him.*
We saw the man. ⟶ *They* saw the man.

In English, at least, the pronoun merely takes the place of the noun in practically all cases without further change of structure. (The notable exception occurs with certain two-part verbs that require a change in word order, e.g., *I called up MY FRIEND*, but *I called HIM up*.) Thus this category is for English merely a subdivision of the preceding category, and truly a mere replacement operation. In many foreign languages this may not be the case. The pronoun may, for instance, take a different position in the sentence than the one occupied by the noun. In that case it would be technically more correct to speak of a pronoun *transformation* than of a pronoun *replacement*.

(3) *Verb replacement:* Replace one verb by another:

Charles *sees* the boy. ⟶ Charles *knows* the boy.
Robert will *follow* orders. ⟶ Robert will *understand* orders.

(4) *Adjective replacement:* Replace one adjective by another:

My *good* friend knows the answer.⟶ My *old* friend knows the answer.

Charles is *lazy.* ⟶ Charles is *intelligent.*

(5) *Adverb replacement:* Replacement of one abverb by another:

Robert works *continuously.* ⟶ Robert works *slowly.*

Charles arrived *late this morning.* ⟶ Charles arrived *early last night.*

Slightly more complicated are the operations that we might call:

B. BASIC EXPANSION OPERATIONS

In these operations you do change the structure of the original sentence somewhat by adding to or expanding one of its original elements. The most important basic expansion operations are:

(6) *Verb expansion:* By this operation we understand simply what the name says, making the verb bigger. For English this would involve some of the procedures described in Part I: (a) replacing the simple form of the verb by have (had) + past participle; (b) putting an auxiliary verb (function word) before the verb; or (c) replacing the verb by the progressive tense (be + -ing form):

Robert *works* all the time. ⟶ Robert *has worked* all the time.

Robert *works* all the time. ⟶ Robert *should work* all the time.

Robert *works* all the time. ⟶ Robert *is working* all the time.

Robert ought to *work.* ⟶ Robert ought to *have worked.*

(7) *Adverbial expansion:* This involves adding to the verb part of the sentence by adding an adverb or adding to an already existing adverb:

Charles *sings.* ⟶ Charles sings *beautifully.*

Charles sings *every day.* ⟶ Charles sings *beautifully every day.*

(8) *Noun expansion:* This operation involves adding to the noun by various means; the most common are by using (additional) modifying adjectives or by prepositional expressions (preposition type function word + noun):

My *friend* is here. ⟶ My *good friend* is here.

I know that *old man*. ⟶ I know that *good, wise old man*.

The *boy* is here. ⟶ The *boy with the papers* is here.

Note that in English the possessive of the noun can of course be used just like a prepositional expression for expanding another noun:

This pen doesn't write. ⟶ *My aunt's pen* doesn't write.

The *leg* is broken. ⟶ The *dog's leg* is broken.

The *leg* is broken. ⟶ The *leg of the chair* is broken.

Another way in which nouns can be expanded in English is by the use of another noun as modifier:

The *bottle* is on the *table*. ⟶ The *milk bottle* is on the *coffee* table.

The next group of important changes are the ones that we might call:

C. SIMPLE TRANSFORMATIONS

These changes involve not just a replacement or expansion of the existing grammatical structure, but a change in the structure itself. The most important of these simple transformations are:

(9) *Change in verb form:* This means replacing the verb form by another. We consider this operation, because of its importance in speaking the language, as a special operation of the transformation type. Notice, however, that from the point of view of English (and many other languages) the change involved is a morphological one rather than a change in the structure of the sentence.

I *speak* to Charles. ⟶ I *spoke* to Charles.

We *know* the answer. ⟶ We *knew* the answer.

Note also that within our classification and for the purpose of discussing English grammar we have classified changes like *I speak English* ⟶ *I can speak English* ⟶ *I have spoken English* ⟶ *I am going to speak English* as verb expansion rather than change in verb form.

(10) *The negative transformation:* This involves making a positive statement negative:

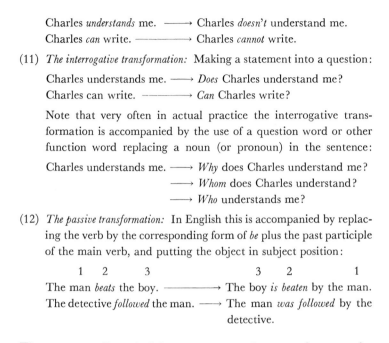

Charles *understands* me. ⟶ Charles *doesn't* understand me.

Charles *can* write. ⟶ Charles *cannot* write.

(11) *The interrogative transformation:* Making a statement into a question:

Charles understands me. ⟶ *Does* Charles understand me?

Charles can write. ⟶ *Can* Charles write?

Note that very often in actual practice the interrogative transformation is accompanied by the use of a question word or other function word replacing a noun (or pronoun) in the sentence:

Charles understands me. ⟶ *Why* does Charles understand me?

⟶ *Whom* does Charles understand?

⟶ *Who* understands me?

(12) *The passive transformation:* In English this is accompanied by replacing the verb by the corresponding form of *be* plus the past participle of the main verb, and putting the object in subject position:

    1 2   3   3   2   1

The man *beats* the boy. ⟶ The boy *is beaten* by the man.

The detective *followed* the man. ⟶ The man *was followed* by the detective.

The most complicated of the sentence creation procedures are the ones that we shall call:

D. SUBORDINATE CLAUSE OPERATIONS

These might also be called the "replacement-transformation" procedures, since what is involved in using the subordinate clause is a transformation as well as a replacement. First of all, we can think of a subordinate clause as a main clause that has been transformed or changed into a subordinate one, and secondly, the clause is used either to replace a noun, or to take the place of an adverb or a noun modifier. At least we can assume that it fits into the place that might have been occupied by one of these. To give an example, we take the sentence *He has told the truth* and transform it into a subordinate clause→*that he has told the truth.* Then we take this clause and fit it, so to speak, into the sentence *I know this fact* by replacing the noun (and its modifier) *this fact* by that clause. Result: *I know that he has told the truth.* The above is an example of a *noun clause.* Other examples would be:

(13) *Noun clause expansion:*

    (a) This is true ⟶ *that this is true*
        [*the truth*] is obvious ⟶ *That this is true* is obvious.

    (b) We understand his objection ⟶ *that we understand his objection*
        I doubt [our understanding] ⟶ I doubt *that we understand his objection.*

(14) *Adverbial clause expansion:* In this procedure a sentence is transformed into an adverbial clause and then fitted into the place of an adverbial modifier.

The moon was shining ⟶ *while the moon was shining.*
Charles worked [late] ⟶ Charles worked *while the moon was shining.*
We answered without thinking ⟶ *because we answered without thinking.*
Robert was upset [by our answer] ⟶ Robert was upset *because we answered without thinking.*

(15) *Relative (adjectival) clause expansion:* Here the subordinate clause is fitted into the place that could have been occupied by a noun modifier:

Charles is my good old friend ⟶ *who is my good old friend*
[Good old] Charles didn't come ⟶ Charles, *who is my good old friend,* didn't come.
Jack's work is not very accurate ⟶ *whose work is not very accurate*
[lazy] Jack didn't win any prize ⟶ Jack, *whose work is not very accurate,* didn't win any prize.

To review the procedure that we have just described, let us take some simple sentences and perform on them the "sentence creation" operations that we have outlined. Let us perform the simple replacement operations (in succession) on the sentence *The boys understand this difficult problem quite well.*

1. The *students* understand this difficult problem quite well.
2. *We*   understand this difficult problem quite well.
3. We   *grasp*   this difficult problem quite well.
4. We   grasp   this *complicated* problem quite well.
5. We   grasp   this complicated problem *very easily.*

Now let us try the simple expansion operations (in succession) on the sentence *We understand the question.*

  6. We *may understand* the question.
  7. We may understand the question *very easily*.
  8. We may understand *our teacher's* question very easily.

We can try the transformation operations in succession on the sentence *He understands the answer.*

  9. He *understood* the answer.
 10. He *didn't* understand the answer.
 11. (Why) didn't he understand the answer?
 12. (Why) wasn't the answer understood by him?

Finally let us take the sentence *He knows English grammar* and try to transform it into a subordinate clause to be fitted into various positions in the sentence: *Charles understands everything clearly.* In other words, let us transform the subordinate clause in such a way that it can be used (1) in place of the subject noun, (2) in place of the object noun, (3) as an adverbial modifier, (4) as an adjectival modifier:

 13. (a) Whoever knows English grammar understands everything clearly.
     (b) Charles understands clearly that he knows English grammar.
 14. Charles understands everything clearly because he knows English grammar.
 15. Charles, who knows English grammar, understands everything clearly.

Another way of reviewing the basic operations is to think of them as the operations that you yourself are using—though unconsciously —all the time, even in your native language, in order to express yourself. The only real difference is that in the foreign language these operations—this conversion of known "raw material" into sentences for self-expression—must, initially at least, be a conscious process. But let us see how it works in the native language.

Someone says *Charles speaks French very well.* And you answer *Yes, but I don't speak it at all.* You can think of this answer as derived from the original statement by the basic operations we have just discussed:

Charles speaks French very well.

(2) *I* speak it very well.

(10) I *don't* speak it very well.

(5) I don't speak it *at all.*

Or another example: *The United States is a powerful country.* Your reaction may be: *I hope that it will always be a powerful and peaceful country.* The steps involved in arriving at your statement would be:

The United States is a powerful country.

(2) *It* is a powerful country.

(6) It *will be* a powerful country.

(7) It will *always* be a powerful country.

(8) It will always be a powerful *and peaceful* country.

(13) I hope *that it will always be a powerful and peaceful country* (i.e., converting the statement into a subordinate clause and fitting it into the sentence "I hope . . .").

We have already stated that in your native language the replacement and transformation operations are rapid, automatic, unconscious. You might think of the way in which you control your native language as a series of such operations performed instantaneously and simultaneously by that wonderful "electronic computer" that operates in the speech areas of your brain. Learning a foreign language means, in the last analysis, teaching this computer the rules that operate in the foreign language, and training it to perform the foreign language operations. The more rapidly, the more easily the computer performs, the more you approach fluency in the foreign language. Once the computer has learned to operate in the foreign language with the same instantaneous, unconscious rapidity that characterizes its function in your native language, then you can truly say that you are speaking the foreign language "like a native."

Learning Exercises

1. Just to show how much meaning can be supplied from context, and to what extent we can rely on guessing the meaning of words, we have taken at random a text and left out some of the lexical items. See whether you can understand the text any-

way, and whether you can supply the missing items or words that approximate their meaning. (The words omitted from the original text are supplied as answers to the exercise.)

"Of Gottfried von Strassburg we only know that he was __(1)__ a native of the __(2)__ for which he is named, that he was not of __(3)__ family, but well educated and apparently in good __(4)__ and that he must have died still __(5)__ young, before 1210. One of the old manuscripts has a __(6)__ , which represents him as a __(7)__ man with long, curling __(8)__ , but its __(9)__ cannot be relied upon. He was perhaps a __(10)__ friend of Hartmann von Aue. It is not known whether he ever __(11)__ Wolfram von Eschenbach. Gottfried also __(12)__ the subject of his one __(13)__, "Tristan," from English and French __(14)__ . It had even been __(15)__ before him by a German poet, Eilhart von Oberg.

Answer: 1. probably 2. city 3. noble 4. circumstances 5. comparatively 6. portrait 7. young 8. locks 9. authenticity 10. personal 11. met 12. drew 13. epic 14. sources 15. used

2. Apply all of the replacement operations (1-5) in succession to each of the following sentences:

(a) My friend will gladly follow your good advice.
(b) Charles has never understood your complicated explanations.

Sample Answer:

(a) My friend will gladly follow your good advice.

   1. My *son* will gladly follow your good advice.
   2. *He*   will gladly follow your good advice.
   3. He   will gladly *seek* your good advice.
   4. He   will gladly seek your *fine* advice.
   5. He   will *always* seek your fine advice.

(b) Charles has never understood your complicated explanations.

   1. Charles has never understood your complicated *actions*.
   2. *He*   has never understood your complicated actions.

3. He   has never   *liked*   your complicated actions.
4. He   has never   liked   your   *strange*   actions.
5. He   has *always*   liked   your   strange   actions.

3. Apply the expansion operations (6-8) in succession to each of the following sentences:

(a) I know the answer.
(b) The boy may succeed.
(c) We know this man.

Sample Answer:

(a) I know the answer.

    6. I *may* know the answer.
    7. I may *never* know the answer.
    8. I may never know the *whole* answer.

(b) The boy may succeed.

    6. The boy may *have succeeded*.
    7. The boy may have succeeded *brilliantly*.
    8. *My friend's* boy may have succeeded brilliantly.

(c) We know this man.

    6. We *have known* this man.
    7. We have known this man *very well*.
    8. We have known this *fine old* man very well.

4. Apply—again in succession—the transformation operations (9-12) to each of the following sentences:

(a) The farmer kills the duckling.
(b) John understands Mary.
(c) The man cheats the girl.

Answer:

(a) The farmer kills the duckling.

    9. The farmer *killed* the duckling.
    10. The farmer *didn't kill* the duckling.
    11. *Didn't* the farmer *kill the duckling?*
    12. *Wasn't the duckling killed by the farmer?*

(b) John understands Mary.

   9. John *understood* Mary.

  10. John *didn't understand* Mary.

  11. *Didn't* John *understand* Mary?

  12. *Wasn't Mary understood by John?*

(c) The man cheats the girl.

   9. The man *cheated* the girl.

  10. The man *didn't cheat* the girl.

  11. *Didn't* the man *cheat* the girl?

  12. *Wasn't the girl cheated by the man?*

5. Transform each of the following sentences into subordinate clauses and use them in the replacement-transformation procedures (13-15):

(a) This is true.

(b) His son is sick.

(c) He is a conceited fool.

Sample Answer:

(a) This is true.

  13. *I know that* this is true.

  14. *He left because* this is true.

  15. *An answer* that is true *must be accepted.*

(b) His son is sick.

  13. *I realize that* his son is sick.

  14. *He is staying here although* his son is sick.

  15. *Charles, whose* son is sick, *won't come to the meeting.*

(c) He is a conceited fool.

  13. That he is a conceited fool *should be obvious to anybody.*

  14. *She loves him although* he is a conceited fool.

  15. *Charles,* who is a conceited fool, *manages to be quite successful.*

6. The following are a series of "statements" and "reaction statements." See whether you can connect them through the replacement, expansion, and transformation operations:

(a) His father was born in Russia.—(No), I am sure that Charles' father was born in Poland.

(b) Robert speaks French.—He can't even speak English.

(c) I want to go to England.—Some day I may want to go to England too.

(d) Do you want to leave?—No, I'll always want to stay.

Answer:

(a) His father was born in Russia.

   1. His father was born in *Poland.*

   8. *Charles'* father was born in Poland.

  15. *I am sure that* Charles' father was born in Poland.

(b) Robert speaks French.

   1. Robert speaks *English.*

   2. *He* speaks English.

   6. He *can speak* English.

  10. He *cannot* speak English.

   7. He cannot *even* speak English.

(c) I want to go to England.

   6. I *may* want to go to England.

   7. *Someday* I may want to go to England *too.*

(d) Do you want to leave?

  10. (in "reverse"). You want to leave.

   2. *I* want to leave.

   3. I want to *stay.*

   6. I *will* want to stay.

   7. I will *always* want to stay.

7. See whether you can apply the counterparts of the fifteen operations that we have discussed in a foreign language. Since the purpose of this book is not to teach any specific foreign language, we cannot of course show in detail how these operations are carried out and discuss all the problems and difficulties that they imply for a specific language. We will, however, illustrate examples in the answers for the following sentences in French, Spanish, and German:

(a) *Successive replacement (operations 1-5):*

> *French:* Mon frèré aîné donne souvent de l'argent à votre cousin.
>
> Spanish: Mi hermano mayor a menudo (le) da dinero a su primo.
>
> German: Mein älterer Bruder gibt oft Ihrem Vetter Geld.

Sample Answer:

French: Mon frère aîné donne souvent de l'argent à votre cousin.

1. Mon frère aîné donne souvent de l'argent à votre oncle.
2. Mon frère aîné lui donne souvent de l'argent.
3. Mon frère aîné lui envoie souvent de l'argent.
4. Mon frère cadet lui envoie souvent de l'argent.
5. Mon frère cadet lui envoie encore de l'argent.

Spanish: Mi hermano mayor a menudo (le) da dinero a su primo.

1. Mi hermano mayor a menudo (le) da dinero a su tío.
2. Mi hermano mayor a menudo le da dinero (a él).
3. Mi hermano mayor a menudo le envia dinero (a él).
4. Mi hermano menor a menudo le envia dinero (a él).
5. Mi hermano menor todavía le envia dinero (a él).

German: Mein älterer Bruder gibt oft Ihrem Vetter Geld.

1. Mein älterer Bruder gibt oft Ihrem Onkel Geld.
2. Mein älterer Bruder gibt ihm oft Geld.
3. Mein älterer Bruder schickt ihm oft Geld.
4. Mein jüngerer Bruder schickt ihm oft Geld.
5. Mein jüngerer Bruder schickt ihm noch Geld.

(b) *Successive expansions (operations 6-8):*

> French: Le professeur cherchait le livre.
> Spanish: El profesor buscaba el libro.
> German: Der Professor suchte das Buch.

Sample Answer:

French: Le professeur cherchait le livre.

6. Le professeur avait cherché le livre.

    7. Le professeur avait cherché le livre ailleurs.

    8. Le vieux professeur de mon ami avait cherché le livre ailleurs.

Spanish: El profesor buscaba el libro.

    6. El profesor había buscado el libro.

    7. El profesor había buscado el libro en otra parte.

    8. El viejo profesor de mi amigo había buscado el libro en otra parte.

German: Der Professor suchte das Buch.

    6. Der Professor hatte das Buch gesucht.

    7. Der Professor hatte das Buch anderswo gesucht.

    8. Der alte Professor meines Freundes hatte das Buch anderswo gesucht.

(c) *Successive transformations (operations 9-12)*:

    French: Le garçon écrit la lettre.
    Spanish: El joven escribe la carta.
    German: Der Junge schreibt den Brief.

Sample Answer:

French: Le garçon écrit la lettre.

    9. Le garçon écrira la lettre.

  10. Le garçon n'écrira pas la lettre.

  11. Le garçon n'écrira-t-il pas la lettre?

  12. La lettre ne sera-t-elle pas écrite par le garçon?

Spanish: El joven escribe la carta.

    9. El joven escribió la carta.

  10. El joven no escribió la carta.

  11. ¿El joven no escribió la carta?

  12. ¿La carta no fue escrita por el joven?

German: Der Junge schreibt den Brief.

    9. Der Junge schrieb den Brief.

  10. Der Junge schrieb den Brief nicht.

  11. Schrieb der Junge den Brief nicht?

  12. Wurde der Brief von dem Jungen nicht geschrieben?

(d) *Subordinate clause operations (operations 13-15)*:

French: Charles a beaucoup d'amis.
Spanish: Carlos tiene muchos amigos.
German: Karl hat viele Freunde.

Sample Answer:

French: Charles a beaucoup d'amis.

13. Je ne crois pas que Charles ait beaucoup d'amis.
14. Quoique Charles ait beaucoup d'amis, il est malheureux.
15. C'est un homme qui a beaucoup d'amis.

Spanish: Carlos tiene muchos amigos.

13. No creo que Carlos tenga muchos amigos.
14. Aunque Carlos tenga muchos amigos, no es felìz.
15. Es un hombre que tiene muchos amigos.

German: Karl hat viele Freunde.

13. Ich glaube nicht, dass Karl viele Freunde hat.
14. Obgleich Karl viele Freunde hat, ist er doch unglücklich.
15. Das ist ein Mann, der viele Freunde hat.

Bibliography

The following works deal with topics discussed in this book, and/or give further access to detailed bibliographies concerned with subjects with which this book is dealing. The bibliography is meant only as a guide for the student seeking further information. Books which require or have the purpose to impart a highly specialized knowledge of linguistics have *not* been included in the bibliography. Books of a somewhat more technical nature are followed by an asterisk (*). Those specifically meant to be popularizations for the layman are followed by the symbol (P).

1. GENERAL LINGUISTICS

BOLINGER, DWIGHT, *Aspects of Language*. New York: Harcourt, Brace & World, Inc., 1968. (P)

DINEEN, FRANCIS P., S.J., *An Introduction to General Linguistics*. New York: Holt, Rinehart & Winston, Inc., 1967.*

GLEASON, H. A., JR., *An Introduction to Descriptive Linguistics* (rev. ed.). New York: Holt, Rinehart & Winston, Inc., 1961.*

HALL, ROBERT A., JR., *Introductory Linguistics*. Philadelphia: Chilton Book Company, 1961.*

HOCKETT, C. F., *A Course in Modern Linguistics*. New York: The Macmillan Company, 1958.*

HUGHES, J. P., *The Science of Language*. New York: Random House, Inc., 1962.

ORNSTEIN, JACOB, AND WILLIAM GAGE, *The ABC's of Language and Linguistics*. Philadelphia: Chilton Book Company, 1964.

PEI, M. A., *An Invitation to Linguistics, A Basic Introduction to the Science of Language*. New York: Doubleday & Co., Inc., 1965. (P)

SAPIR, EDWARD, *Language: An Introduction to the Study of Speech*. New York: Harcourt, Brace & World, Inc., 1921 (Paperback edition: Harvest Books).

2. STRUCTURE OF ENGLISH

FRIES, C. C., *The Structure of English, An Introduction to the Construction of English Sentences*. New York: Harcourt, Brace & World, Inc., 1952.

JACOBS, RODERICK, AND PETER S. ROSENBAUM, *English Transformational Grammar*. Waltham, Mass.: Blaisdell Publishing Company, 1968.

ROBERTS, PAUL, *English Sentences*. New York: Harcourt, Brace & World, Inc., 1962.

————, *Modern Grammar*. New York: Harcourt, Brace & World, Inc., 1968.

SLEDD, JAMES A., *A Short Introduction to English Grammar*. Chicago: Scott, Foresman & Company, 1959.

THOMAS, OWEN, *Transformational Grammar and the Teacher of English*. New York: Holt, Rinehart & Winston, Inc., 1965.

3. LANGUAGE LEARNING AND TEACHING

BROOKS, N., *Language and Language Learning, Theory and Practice* (2nd ed.). New York: Harcourt, Brace & World, Inc., 1964.

GRITTNER, FRANK M., *Teaching Foreign Languages.* New York: Harper & Row, Publishers, 1969.

HALL, ROBERT A., JR., *New Ways to Learn a Foreign Language.* New York: Bantam Books, Inc., 1966. (P)

HUGHES, JOHN P., *Linguistics and Language Teaching.* New York: Random House, Inc., 1968.

LADO, R., *Language Teaching, A Scientific Approach.* New York: McGraw-Hill Book Company, 1964.

MOULTON, WILLIAM G., *A Linguistic Guide to Language Learning.* New York: Modern Language Association of America, 1966.

OLIVA, PETER F., *The Teaching of Foreign Languages.* Englewood Cliffs, N.J.: Prentice-Hall, Inc., 1969.

PALMER, H. E., *The Scientific Study and Teaching of Languages.* New York: Harcourt, Brace & World, Inc., 1917.

PEI, MARIO, *How to Learn Language and What Languages to Learn.* New York: Harper & Row, Publishers, 1966. (P)

RIVERS, WILGA M., *Teaching Foreign Language Skills.* Chicago: University of Chicago Press, 1969.

4. LANGUAGE TEACHING AND APPLIED LINGUISTICS

French:

BELASCO, S., AND A. VALDMAN, *Applied Linguistics: French.* Boston: D. C. Heath & Company, 1961.

MARTY, F., *Linguistics Applied to the Beginning French Course.* Roanoke, Va.: Audio-Visual Publications, 1963.

POLITZER, R. L., *Teaching French, An Introduction to Applied Linguistics* (2nd ed.). Waltham, Mass.: Blaisdell Publishing Company, 1965.

Spanish:

BELASCO, S., AND D. CARDENAS, *Applied Linguistics: Spanish.* Boston: D. C. Heath & Company, 1961.

BULL, W. E., *Spanish for Teachers, Applied Linguistics.* New York: The Ronald Press Co., 1965.

POLITZER, R. L., AND C. N. STAUBACH, *Teaching Spanish, A Linguistic Orientation* (2nd ed.). Waltham, Mass.: Blaisdell Publishing Company, 1965.

STOCKWELL, ROBERT P., AND J. DONALD BOWEN, *The Sounds of English and Spanish.* Chicago: University of Chicago Press, 1965.*

STOCKWELL, ROBERT P., J. DONALD BOWEN, AND JOHN W. MARTIN, *The Grammatical Structures of English and Spanish.* Chicago: University of Chicago Press, 1965.*

German:

BELASCO, S., AND J. W. MARCHAND, *Applied Linguistics: German.* Boston: D. C. Heath & Company, 1961.

KUFNER, H. L., *The Grammatical Structures of English and German.* Chicago: University of Chicago Press, 1962.*

MOULTON, W. G., *The Sounds of English and German.* Chicago: University of Chicago Press, 1962.*

POLITZER, R. L., *Teaching German, A Linguistic Orientation.* Waltham, Mass: Blaisdell Publishing Company, 1968.

5. PSYCHOLOGY OF LANGUAGE LEARNING

RIVERS, W. M., *The Psychologist and the Foreign Language Teacher.* Chicago: University of Chicago Press, 1964.